SEMPERVIVUM

A Gardener's

Perspective of the

Not-So-Humble

Hens-and-Chicks

KEVIN C. VAUGHN

Schiffer Publishing Ltd®

4880 Lower Valley Road • Atglen, PA 19310

Designed by Danielle D. Farmer
Cover design by Molly Shields
Type set in EdelSans/Brandon Grotesque

ISBN: 978-0-7643-5512-7
Printed in China

Published by Schiffer Publishing, Ltd.
4880 Lower Valley Road
Atglen, PA 19310
Phone: (610) 593-1777; Fax: (610) 593-2002
E-mail: Info@schifferbooks.com
Web: www.schifferbooks.com

For our complete selection of fine books on this and related subjects, please visit our website at www.schifferbooks.com. You may also write for a free catalog.

Schiffer Publishing's titles are available at special discounts for bulk purchases for sales promotions or premiums. Special editions, including personalized covers, corporate imprints, and excerpts, can be created in large quantities for special needs. For more information, contact the publisher.

We are always looking for people to write books on new and related subjects. If you have an idea for a book, please contact us at proposals@schifferbooks.com.

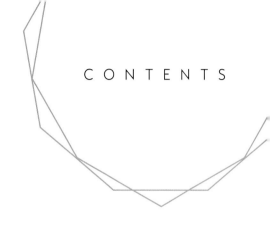

C O N T E N T S

PREFACE

In 1964, my parents were beginning to landscape their property in Athol, Massachusetts, putting in brick walls on one side of the property and more rustic stone walls in an area that ran through a wooded area. Polly Bishop, who lived about a mile away, saw these efforts and offered to share plants from her garden to under-plant and over-plant these walls. When my mom went to Polly's garden to choose some irises and poppies, I tagged along and was just in awe. Polly had a large garden, and the centerpiece was a 200 ft. X 40 ft. ovular garden in which the paths were bordered in stones and the paths were sunken. The irises and poppies were magnificent, but what fascinated me were the hundreds of *Sempervivum* hybrids growing along the paths and among the rocks. I had seen the "green one" that everyone grew, but here were reds, purples, velvety ones, and cobwebbed types. Just amazing! Polly had about 300 different cultivars—almost all that were available in the US at that time. Besides the main garden, Polly had an area that was planted in rows that included her iris seedlings. When she described how these iris seedlings were created I became really excited. I had never met anyone that actually created new plants. How cool was that?

Sensing my interest in the "semps," Polly brought a bunch of her best varieties to plant along the walls at my folks' property. I was really hooked then.

One day, about a month after the iris season visit, I was riding by Polly's garden and saw her out making crosses of the *Sempervivum* and pulled my bicycle in for a look. After Polly demonstrated what she was doing, she said, "Come back tomorrow and you can make your own crosses." You do not have to ask a young science nerd that twice! Patty Drown was another neighbor, and was also into science. Her aunt Millie sent her a monthly science kit that was a highlight of the month for us, and we would quickly perform all the experiments. We both collected insects, rocks, and leaves, as we lived in the country and there were all sorts of wonderful things to explore. Anyway, I knew Patty would be into the *Sempervivums* too, and we arrived early the next morning to start making crosses. The *Sempervivum* were blooming at near peak and several of the very best hybrids were blooming. It was such fun to use the little muslin bags to protect our crosses from insects and to dab the pollen from one cultivar on to the stigmas of the other. We made a number of different crosses, and as the stalks dried, we harvested the dust-like seed in September. Patty constructed a small seedling bed and I planted my seed behind clumps of daylilies and irises so they would not be disturbed. The next spring, as I was walking through Patty's garden, I noticed these tiny, cobwebbed seedlings in one of the neat rows. I grabbed Patty and we were so excited. That was the first sight of the plant that became 'Denise's Cobweb' (named for her sister!). After seeing those seedlings, I noticed mine were also germinating. For a first try at hybridizing I was extremely lucky: the hybrids 'Silvertone,' 'Emerald Spring,' and 'Greenwich Time' came from that first batch of seedlings. The latter two still grace my garden fifty-three years later. Pat's 'Denise's Cobweb' is here too, and would become an important parent for me in further breeding.

Massachusetts was a hot bed of horticultural interest, and Polly was connected to many of the people in this world. People were so generous and encouraging to this literal "new kid on the block," and soon I had large collections of irises of all types, hosta, and of course, semps. PhDs would visit my yard, and my dad once commented, "you certainly have a lot of little old ladies as friends!" Bill Nixon started visiting around 1969, and we shared many of the plants that became the basis of his collection. Winnie Crane, wife of the owner of Crane Paper (they make the paper for dollar bills!), had a lovely piece of property in Dalton, Massachusetts, including large pieces of driftwood that were planted with semps like living sculptures. Lunch in her enormous mansion was certainly impressive for a sixteen-year-old kid! The state of the names on the semps at that stage were greatly confused, and to sort them out Winnie set aside a large area for a test planting. Each of the nurseries from the US selling semps was encouraged to send a representative of their particular cultivar, and we used plants from Peter Mitchell's collection in the UK as the reference standard. Each cultivar was planted in squares with identical potting mix with the reference cultivar. The plants were evaluated over several seasons and included careful examination of the characteristics of each plant. The correct plants were then sent to each nursery. This greatly helped identity, but at that time there were not even a tenth of what we have now. Still, it was good to have the names correct, at least briefly!

By 1970, I had produced a number of seedlings that I felt were worthy of introduction. Helen Payne's Oakhill Gardens was one of the premier nurseries at that time, and her catalog was the most extensive of any in the US. She agreed to introduce my cultivars to the market. I remember vividly a phone call from Helen shortly after she received plants of my 'Jungle Shadows' and 'Lipstick.' In her obvious excitement she said, "Kevin, we can sell *lots* of those two!" And indeed she did. My plants were now known around the world, and I was surprised to find that most of them are still offered for sale even today. The two plants that Helen lauded as quite special went on to win awards in the UK. Not bad for a teenager! From these early phases of my crossing program, about forty different hybrids were brought to market.

Long before the days of the internet, communication between plant enthusiasts was much more limited, especially if you lived far from horticultural hot beds. I started a round robin, a correspondence group where each of the participants would write letters, posing questions, and then pass it on to another. It was a *slow* process, with only a couple appearances of these letters each year. It did allow for contact between many of us interested in *Sempervivum* in the US. The round robin became the nucleus of what became the Sempervivum Fancier's Association.

My associations with plants changed my life. I studied genetics and botany, ending up with a PhD in botany with emphasis in genetics from Miami (OH) University. After finishing my PhD, I had a long and successful career with the USDA in Mississippi studying weeds. Mississippi was not a good place to grow *Sempervivum*, although I did manage to grow a few in stone troughs in the yard and in pots in my growth chamber at work. Although the semps were not as happy in Mississippi, I hybridized irises, daylilies, and daffodils instead, filling two long backyards with plants.

Retiring to Oregon in 2010, I started with semps again. Even before I had arrived in Oregon, I ordered a number of semps so that they would be ready to plant when I arrived! Can you tell I was anxious to get back into growing and hybridizing them? Crosses were made on the first year plants, and now I am growing thousands of seedlings and introducing new cultivars each year. Upon arriving in Oregon, I discovered a marvelous group of local enthusiasts, chief among them Lynn Smith and Cynda Foster. Both have unbridled enthusiasm for semps, and Lynn is one of the directors of the Sempervivum chat group on the National Gardening Association (NGA) website. For several years now members of that chat group have descended upon Salem for a "clinic" that involves garden visits, a class on evaluating cultivars and hybridizing techniques, and a fun banquet at the end. One thing everyone at this meeting and in the NGA chat group comments on is the lack of a book on semps. Much of the information that I knew was really never recorded in printed form, or was only found in long, obsolete price lists and catalogs. It needed to be preserved in a place for future generations. That was the impetus for this book.

I have written this book for gardeners. This is not a taxonomic discussion of the group, as most of the species plants have been surpassed by the work of hybridizers, or are plants that require special conditions to keep them from rotting. Instead, the book concentrates on the culture of the plants, their many uses in the garden, and the species plants still worth growing, plus some of the history of the people and plants, some of my choices of cultivars, and instructions on how to make your own hybrids. I hope it will be a book that a beginner can pick up and learn the basics, but also a book that will have lots of good information for aficionados as well. For aficionados, I have added tidbits about the personalities and details of hybridizing and raising plants from seed.

In writing this book, I have been fortunate to meet a whole other group of people with whom I have known by name or correspondence and have now met in person. These new acquaintances are just wonderful people. Plant people tend to be the most interesting types of people, too. They definitely have opinions! For me, the people that I have met through my horticultural interests are my greatest gifts, even more than my treasured plants.

Lastly, I want to thank all of the many people that have contributed photos to this volume, including Howard Wills, Ray Stephenson, Janis Noyes (and a wonderful lunch learning about the history of Squaw Mountain Gardens), Don Mylin, Mark Brandhorst, Matts Jopson, Lynn Smith, Dave Jerell, Chris Rentmeister, Chris Hansen, Ella May Wulf (and her brother-in-law photographer, Alan), Erwin Geiger, Bev Richards, Beatrix Bodmeier, and Greg Colucci. The family of Winnie Crane generously supplied a photo of her. The wonderful website of George Mendl has many wonderful pictures and stories; George allowed me to download several of his images for use in this book. It took a village to bring this book together!

KEVIN VAUGHN
Salem, Oregon

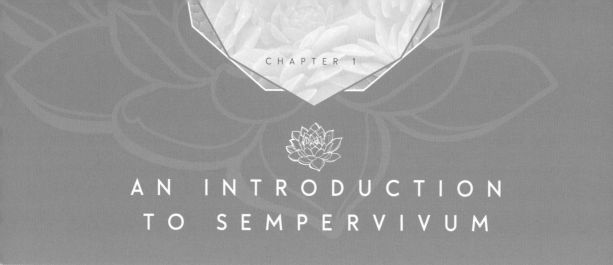

CHAPTER 1

AN INTRODUCTION TO SEMPERVIVUM

WHAT ARE *SEMPERVIVUM*?

Sempervivum have long fascinated botanists and gardeners. One reason for this fascination is the form of the plant. The *Sempervivum* plant is a ground-hugging succulent rosette, a tight clustering of fleshy, evergreen leaves arranged in a way that resemble a double rose flower. In many ways *Sempervivum* rosettes resemble tiny chunky cabbages or artichokes. Children especially seem to be intrigued by these plants, and it is my own childhood fascination that endears me to these plants to this day.

Fig. 1-1. A rosette of a green semp seedling of the author's showing stolons with offset rosettes.

The genus *Sempervivum* is a member of the Crassulaceae family, which includes such other common succulent garden plants as the sedums and the greenhouse plants *Aeonium* and *Kalanchoe*. Recent genetic analysis indicate that the *Sempervivum* are a newly-formed group (and still evolving), and probably originated from a group of species in the genus *Sedum*. The most current revision of the genus *Sempervivum* contains about forty-five species (t'Hart et al. 2003). Like other succulent plants, *Sempervivum* plants store large reserves of water in their cells and have a thick, waxy cuticle to retain the water. This water storage capacity allows these plants to survive during prolonged periods of drought, although not as well as most species of cactus that are even more highly drought-tolerant.

Most *Sempervivum* species are plants of the mountains, growing in and amongst crevices in rocks and other places inhospitable to most plants. One species of *Sempervivum* is found in the Atlas Mountains of Morocco, several more are found in the mountain regions in Spain, and there are a great number of species indigenous in the Alps and Balkans. Another group of species grow as far east as Turkey and the Elburz Mountains of Iran. Most of the species are found in the Alps and Balkans; it is from these areas that the species used to make hybrids have mostly come, as these species are the most tolerant of diverse gardening conditions.

Although most of the wild *Sempervivum* species are green, hybridizers have greatly increased the colors of the rosette, adding shades of gold, orange, all shades of red, and purples from palest lavender to nearly black. Many of these leaves have patterns of color distribution either concentrated at the tip or base, multicolored, and with lighter watermarks.

Fig. 1-2. A semp seedling of the author's with blue-green leaves marked in red.

◄ **Fig. 1-3.** A lime seedling of the author's with velvety texture.

◄ **Fig. 1-4.** 'Aalrika,' a beautiful rosette with many shades of reds, oranges, and purple.

◄ **Fig. 1-5.** 'Lipstick,' a bright red with velvety leaves.

Fig. 1-6. A mustard colored seedling of the author's.

The leaves themselves are quite variable too, with some cultivars having wide, squatty leaves and others having long and sharply pointed ones. Sizes of the rosettes range from rosettes about ¼ in. in diameter to over a foot. Virtually every combination of leaf length, shape, and size are found within the cultivars. Besides these sizes and colors, one of the species, *S. arachnoideum*, has contributed a most unusual structure to its cultivars and hybrids: extensive plant hairs at the leaf terminus that coalesce to form a cobweb-like netting over the surface of the rosette. This cobweb probably serves two functions: it protects the rosettes from the strong rays of the summer sun and the pectin-enriched hairs may be useful in collecting dew during periods of low rainfall. Many of the hybrids of cobwebbed to non-cobwebbed types do not have a full cobweb, but rather a tuft of hair on the tip. Other species and cultivars have a velvety texture to the leaf that adds a depth of color to the reds and purples, or cilia along the leaf edge that give a frosted effect. By using these species, hybridizers have created around 7,000 cultivars. Today's gardener has never had it better with this huge diversity of plants to grace our gardens. Although the *Sempervivum* cultivars of my youth were dominated by relatively uninteresting green or muddy plants, today the colors, patterns, and variety of sizes and leaf shapes is truly dazzling.

Part of the fascination of *Sempervivum* is that their looks tend to change over the course of the season. This involves changes in the form of the rosette, its size, and the colors or patterns in the leaf. Some, like the cultivar 'Killer,' can be red, purple, green, or green with red leaf bases depending on the season. Helen Payne (1972) described this charmingly by writing it is "like seeing your best girl in a dress, then in shorts, then gussied up for a dance." Very well put!

Fig. 1-7. Details of the cobweb.

Linnaeus gave these plants the genus name *Sempervivum*, which is Latin for "always living," referring to the ability of these plants to grow in some rather hostile environments and the ability of these plants to reproduce vegetatively. Most *Sempervivum* species reproduce by means of stolons (lateral stems), shoots that are capable of producing a new plant—an offset—at the stolon terminus. This plant umbilical cord allows the new plantlet to draw nutrients from the mother rosette until the offset has grown sufficiently to grow on its own. The "roller type" *Sempervivum* makes very thin stolons, so that these tiny plants actually fall from the plant and root wherever they lay. This habit of a large rosette surrounded by numerous small rosette clones has given rise to one of the popular names for this group of plant, "hen(s)-and-chickens." Despite this rather rough start on its own, the rollers are able to make plants and grow quite happily. A third type of vegetative propagation is found in *S. heuffelii*, in which the crown appears to split into divisions. Zonneveld (1981) believes that this so-called crown division is really a variation of the stolon type, but one in which the stolons are very short and stout. Occasionally, *Sempervivum* that normally produce offsets on long stolons will also crown divide in support of this view.

Sempervivum are not deeply rooted, although they generally have a long tap root that is able to penetrate into tiny crevices in rock so that the plants may survive in even the tiniest patches of soil in their native mountains. The gardener can use this ability to grow in less soil to put plants in small crevices in dry walls and in other areas where little soil is available to support a plant.

Fig. 1-8. A mix of different roller cultivars.

➤ **Fig. 1-9.** A roller seedling of the author's with prominent red-purple leaf tips.

◀ **Fig. 1-10.** A bright red *S. heuffelii* seedling.

FLOWERS AND SEEDS

Unlike most garden plants, *Sempervivum* are not grown for their flowers, although some do have quite attractive ones. Ironically, *Sempervivum*, the "live forever" plant, is actually monocarpic. That is, when it blooms it actually dies. Plants generally do not bloom until their third or fourth year of growth, so the plant has achieved a relatively large size for that cultivar. Moreover, over the course of that time, the rosette has produced new rosettes on stolons for one or two seasons, so the blooming rosette has reproduced itself many fold before blooming. The roller types and the species *S. calcareum* and its cultivars bloom much more rarely. Generally, the plant gives the gardener a clue that it is about to flower. The first indication is a more intense color of the rosette about to bloom compared to others in the clump. The next obvious symptom is the early elongation of the center of the rosette, indicating that the bloomstalk is forming. Flower stalks are five to eight inches tall on the smaller rosettes, but can be as big as two feet on some of the bigger plants.

Fig. 1-11. A cobweb type with a bloomstalk emerging in several rosettes.

Flower colors range from white through yellow and cream, and a large number have pinkish to deep rose flowers. Most flowers are smallish (½ in. in diameter), but some, such as 'Othello' and 'Pacific Spring Mist,' have larger flowers that make more of a garden statement. The flowers of the majority of species are open, star-like flowers with ten to fifteen petals and with as many as sixty flowers (and occasionally much more) on a branched stalk. The flowers start to bloom on the interior of the stalk and bloom in sequence to the tips; flowering times are up to a month or more. The species and hybrids in the *Jovibarba* subsection have a more campanulate flower form with six fringed petals, with flowers in creams to yellows, and the stalk tends to be less extensive than in the other *Sempervivum* species.

All of the species are well-visited by a variety of insects and are favorites of honey bees and bumblebees in my garden. I wonder what *Sempervivum* honey tastes like? In New England, Bill Nixon found that a species of solitary bee called the carpenter bee (*Xylocopa virginica*) was the most prominent pollinator of the semps (Nixon 1988).

➤ **Fig. 1-12.** Nearly white flowers on a *S. heuffelii* seedling.

◄ **Fig. 1-13.** A fly robbing pollen on a *Sempervivum* flower.

Occasionally, I see butterflies and skippers visiting the flowers too. The bumblebee seems the most adept at fertilizing the *heuffelii* types based upon their visits to these flowers in my garden, as their long proboscis allows them to collect nectar deep in the flower. Flies that mimic bees are frequent pollen robbers too, although they may also pollinate in the process.

Many gardeners feel the bloomstalks detract from the looks of the *Sempervivum* clump and will either cut off the stalks or remove the entire plant from the clump. The shorter stalks on many of the cobwebbed *Sempervivum* are quite attractive, and all *Sempervivum* flowers are a good source of nectar for bees. As the flowers begin to fade, the entire stalk begins to dry and the seed capsules mature.

The seed are in narrow follicles, and as the stalk dries these follicles split along a suture line, allowing for seed dispersal. The brown seed is minute, and is easily dispersed by the wind. Most growers cut off the bloomstalks before this point so that seedlings are not scattered throughout the garden, contaminating named varieties. Of course, it is great fun to grow *Sempervivum* from seed, especially through careful crossing. (Techniques for doing this are described in chapter 5.) Be warned though, this can be an addiction.

Fig. 1-14. Seed of *S. pittonii*.

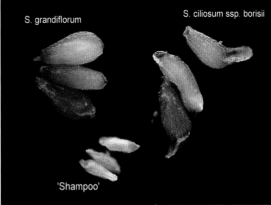

Fig. 1-15. Seeds.

GARDEN USES

Their hardy nature and ease of growth have endeared the *Sempervivum* to gardeners. In chapter 2, many of the ways in which these plants may be used in garden situations are detailed. If you live in areas from Zone 8 and colder, at least a few *Sempervivum* should be one of your go-to gardening plants. Because they thrive even on neglect, these are the ideal plants for a gardener with little time or space in which to garden. Many of my friends grow *Sempervivum* in flats or pots on their balconies. *Sempervivum's* one requirement is decent drainage and not to be planted too deeply. *Sempervivum* were on my mother's list of plants "any fool could grow." This is not far from the truth. The uses of *Sempervivum* are nearly infinite. Every time I think I have seen every possible use, a new one shows its head.

TAXONOMY, SCIENTIFIC AND COMMON NAMES, MYTHOLOGY, AND MEDICAL USES

Besides giving *Sempervivum* its genus name, Linnaeus also named four species. The species named by Linnaeus have stood the test of time, but there has been great confusion since then. The reasons for this are many. In the Alps, five species (*S. tectorum*, *S. grandiflorum*, *S. arachnoideum*, *S. wulfenii*, and *S. montanum*) cross with each other, and many of the hybrids between these species are also fertile. When botanists found these hybrids, they assigned them new species names, creating all sorts of confusion. The great Swiss horticulturalist Correvon (1924) described over 200 such "species." Moreover, botanical gardens distributed seed of species, not knowing that the plants had crossed in their gardens, leading to confusion for the recipients of the seed. Praeger (1932) was the first to make sense of these complexities and which ones were in fact true species. We owe him a debt of gratitude for making a major step in sorting out the nomenclature of this group. Although the ability of *Sempervivum* species to cross has caused many problems for taxonomists, it has been a great boon to hybridizers and gardeners. Most of the species intercross (Smith 1975), and many of the subsequent hybrids are also fertile. Hybridizers have been able to combine characteristics from several species into hybrids in most wonderful ways.

The roller type of *Sempervivum* and the crown-dividing *S. heuffelii* have often been grouped in a separate genus called *Jovibarba*, and you will see many publications that keep them as a separate genus. The most recent taxonomic revision of the group (t'Hart et al. 2003) does keep all of the species in a single genus, relegating *Jovibarba* to a section within the genus *Sempervivum*. Although the rosettes of the *Jovibarba* section resemble those of other members of the genus, the flowers are distinctly campanulate and have fringed petal edges. These species will cross with other members of the genus, although with difficulty, and the hybrids are often malformed. The rollers and *S. heuffelii* will cross with each other to give mostly sterile hybrids; crosses between the rollers give fully fertile hybrids.

The confusion with names was not limited to botanists observing them in the field, either. Because of their propensity to cross, seeds from species that were distributed by botanic gardens often did not produce that same species. Cultivars also became confused when seed from the cultivars were allowed to fall among the clump and were then distributed as that clone. The situation was so confused in the 1970s that a special project was set up at Mrs. Bruce Crane's Sugar Hill Nursery in Dalton, Massachusetts. Plants from all the nurseries were grown under controlled conditions together with reference plants obtained from England. Over 300 cultivars and species selections were examined; 230 cultivars were found to be correct, but another group was so confused they were tossed out as being too difficult to reconcile. Can you imagine such a project now with 7,000 cultivars? Luckily, there are groups in the US and Europe that constantly monitor the offerings of nurseries, and now it is much more likely that a correct plant can be obtained from a nursery with the "Sempervivum Police" working to keep things straight.

Linnaeus may have given the genus name *Sempervivum*, but opinions differ as to its pronunciation! Helen Payne (1972) pronounced it semp-er-VY-vum, whereas I was brought up saying semp-er-VEE-vum. However one pronounces it, anyone into gardening will immediately know to which plants you are referring! Mina Neil (1981) wrote this charming little poem for someone struggling to pronounce *Sempervivum*:

Oh fee, oh fie
To those who harbor
The so ubiquitous Jovibarba
"That way lies madness" these folk say.
But madness lies the other way.
If you have them, never leave 'em
Semper fidelis, Sempervivum.

One might notice that a Boston accent (where terminal "r"s are frequently dropped) is required to get "harbor" and *Jovibarba* to rhyme!

Sempervivum have been gardening and medicinal plants since Biblical times, and this long history has also generated many common names. In Europe, they are often referred to as "houseleeks" and were used on roofs at least since the Middle Ages as a charm against

Fig. 1-16. Ancient print showing the custom of planting semps on the roof as a charm against lightning.

lightning; the Holy Roman Emperor Charlemagne even decreed that all the roofs of buildings should have *Sempervivum* planted on them. I was always confused by the name "houseleeks," as the *Sempervivum* rosette looks more like a tiny cabbage than a leek. However, the Welch name for plant is "leac," so the term houseleek literally means "house plant" or "plant on a house." Linnaeus named the most commonly planted species on roofs as *Sempervivum tectorum*; *tectorum* is "roof" in Latin. In the United States, *Sempervivum* are most often called "hens-and-chickens," as the mother rosette and its numerous offsets give the appearance of a mother hen and her chicks placed around her. Many of the aficionados refer to them simply as "semps." It falls off the lips rather easily! It is what I use, and I will use this throughout much of this book. The subgenus *Jovibarba* (t'Hart et al. 2003) literally translates as "Jupiter's beard," one of the many common names for all of the *Sempervivum*. The term Jupiter's beard refers to the bloomstalk, which has a vague resemblance to a beard, and of course Jupiter (or Thor, if you were from Nordic regions) was associated with lightning. There are long lists of other common names for these plants. Almost any country in which these plants are grown has resulted in a novel name. One of the most strange is "Welcome Home Husband However Drunk You May Be."

Besides their use as charms against lightning, *Sempervivum* have long been used in medicine, chiefly as a fresh juice squeezed from the leaves. It is used to pack on wounds, sores, and burns, as well as to relieve the pain and sting of insect bites and earaches (Pieroni et al. 2003). This is a similar practice to that used in this country with leaves of the succulent plant *Aloe*. Drinking tea made from these extracts has even been used as an ulcer treatment (Bremness 1988).

Like many of these folk cures, there is some scientific basis for the healing power of these extracts. *Sempervivum* leaves have prominent tannin cells which contain concentrations of anti-microbial phenolics (Fahn 1974). These phenolics have been isolated and purified by a number of laboratories, and the antimicrobial and antioxidant nature of these molecules has been demonstrated (Abram and Donko 1999; Kerry et al. 1992; Sentjurc et al. 2003). Glycosides of the flavone kaempferol are the major flavonoid of *S. tectorum* (Alberti et al. 2008; Sentjurc et al. 2003), as well as *S. globiferum* (Szewczyk et al. 2014). The proanthocyanidin delphinidol and the tannin epigallocatechin-3-gallate have both been detected as major compounds in *S. tectorum* leaves, and both are known antimicrobial agents (Abram and Donko 1999).

Sempervivum perform a form of photosynthesis called crassulasic acid metabolism (CAM) that is found in many succulent plants (Wagner and Larcher 1981). Plants accumulate large amounts of malic acid in their vacuoles that would give the leaves a rather acid taste, making them less appealing to would-be herbivores. A friend in Salem described one of his childhood experiences with *Sempervivum*. Thinking that the *Sempervivum* look much like an artichoke, he took a big bite out of one. Much to his dismay, it tasted nothing like an artichoke, but left a disgusting taste in his mouth. Lesson learned! Some herbivores have less disdain for them than humans, although they are clearly not the first choice of most.

REFERENCES

Abram V, M Donko (1999) Tentative identification of polyphenols in *Sempervivum tectorum* and assessment of the antimicrobial activity of *Sempervivum* L. J Agric Food Chem 47: 485-489

Alberti A, B Blazics, A Kery (2008) Evaluation of *Sempervivum tectorum* L. flavonoids by LC and LC-MS. *Chromatographia* (suppl) 68: 107-111

Bremness L (1988) *The Complete Book of Herbs*. Dorling Kindersley Ltd. London, UK

Correvon H (1924) *Les Joubarbes. Imprimerie Medicale & Scientifique*, Brussels, Belgium

Fahn A (1974) *Plant Anatomy*, 2nd edition. Pergamon Press. Oxford, UK

Kerry A, A Blazovics, N Rozlosnik, J Feher, G Petri (1992) "Antioxidative properties of extracts of *S. tectorum*." *Planta Medica* 58 (suppl): 661–66

Neil M (1981) untitled poem. *Sempervivum Fanciers Association Newsletter* 7(3): 16

Nixon C. W. (1988) "Pollinating bee for semps." *Sempervivum Fancier's Association Newsletter* 9: 16

Payne HE (1972) *Plant Jewels of the High Country*. Pine Cone Publishers. Medford, Oregon

Pieroni A, ME Giusti, H Munz, C Lenzarini, G Turkovic, A Turkovic (2003) "Ethnobotanical knowledge of the Istro-Romanians of Zejane in Croatia." *Filoterapia* 74: 710–719

Praegar L (1932) *An Account of the Sempervivum Group*. Royal Horticultural Society, London, UK

Sentjurc M., M Nemec, HD Connor, V Abram (2003) "Antioxidant activity of *Sempervivum tectorum* and its components." *J Agric Food Chem* 51: 2766–2771

Szewczyk K, T Krzaczek, T Lopatynski, U Gawlik-Dziki, C Zidorn (2014) "Flavonoids from *Jovibarba globifera* (Crassulaceae) rosette leaves and their antioxidant activity." *Natural Prod Res* 28: 1655-1658

t'Hart H, B Bleij, B Zonneveld (2003) *Sempervivum* In: Crassulaceae (U Eggli, ed), pp 332–349. Springer Verlag, Berlin

Wagner J., W Larcher (1981) "Dependence of CO_2 gas exchange and acid metabolism of the alpine CAM plant *Sempervivum montanum* on temperature and light." *Oecologia* 50: 88–93

Zonneveld BJM (1981) "An analysis of the process of vegetative propagation in *Jovibarba heuffelii*." *Sempervivum Fanciers Association Newsletter* 7(3): 13–16

CHAPTER 2

CULTURE AND USES OF SEMPERVIVUM IN THE GARDEN

General Information for Growth in the Garden

CHOOSING THE SITE AND CREATING THE GARDEN

Although semps are some of the easiest plants for the gardener to grow, using a few simple rules will give much better results. You will have more increase, and larger, more beautiful rosettes. Correvon (1929) objected to this unnatural, lush growth, as he wanted them to appear as they did in crevices in rocks—more starved. Accordingly, he maintained a separate collection grown in rather lean soil that would be typical of how they grew in the Alps. Most people I find are delighted in growing beautiful, large, and healthy rosettes that show the potential of each cultivar. This is especially true in the summer, when withered and unhappy plants are not a good look in the landscape.

If you live in USDA Zones 8 and lower, there should be at least some semps that will grow in your garden, and in certain areas, you should be able to grow all of the species and hybrids, given a few basic rules.

The first of these rules is *good drainage*. Semps are not bog plants, so you need to find a garden spot where water does not accumulate; growing plants in these wetter areas will lead to rotting of the rosettes and ultimate failure of your planting. You want to choose a site that is raised above the general soil level for best results, so that even after heavy rains there is no puddling of water around the plants. Mounding, creating berms, or creating fully raised beds are the easiest way to achieve this if your garden situation is relatively flat. Oddly, semps prefer to grow on a flat but raised surface for best results. Plants on a slope seem to suffer from soil from above washing over them and the rosettes grow asymmetrically. In my garden, I construct raised beds using pavers that are four inches high and stacked two deep. Because I have a rather long reach, I construct my beds so they are six feet across. If you have shorter arms than I do, determine how far you can reach from the edge of the bed, as you do not want to step in the bed to weed or move plants after it is finally constructed. Fill the bed with soil and allow it to settle before planting. My friend Lynn Smith uses a similar system, but uses larger cement blocks that make for a taller bed. These are filled with soil and make for a higher raised bed than I use, but has the advantage that it requires no stooping to maintain the bed. The pockets at the edge of the bed created by the holes in the cement blocks are perfect sites for smaller semps and rollers which might otherwise spill around the bed.

Fig. 2-1. A bed of semps constructed from cement blocks.

If you happen to garden in an area where the soil is sandy loam, you already have the perfect growing medium for semps. Add a bit of compost or other organic matter to soils such as these and you are ready for planting. Semps are *not* cactus, so make sure that the soil has some ability to retain moisture as well. We are talking sandy *loam*, not sand. If you have heavier soils enriched in clay, adding organic matter is still a good idea. Adding some fine gravel to heavy clays is another effective way to increase the ability of the soil to drain and will require less frequent replacement than organic matter. Another plan is just to buy a good light garden soil and use it to fill the raised bed. Although more pricey, you will almost be assured of a good result. Although some species, such as *S. calcareum*, grow on limestone, these same species seem to do fine in garden situations in which the soil is acidic. The soil in the cavities in rocks in which semps grow is quite acidic, despite what rock surrounds the colony of semps (Raes 2014). In fact, the pH that was measured in these soils was 4.5, more like what would grow good blueberries! The soil mix that I use is about pH 6.0, and the growth of semps is very good in this mix. In Polly Bishop's garden, she mulched her paths with pine needles and she often noted that the semps would be bigger and happier near the pine needles than in the bed. The bit more acidic condition provided by the needles may have contributed to this difference in growth.

The second consideration is *light*. Most often semps are grown in full sun, and the farther North you are, the more light you want to provide your plants. In these types of exposure, even in the North, the plants do not look all that happy during the hottest days of the summer. The rosettes tend to draw up and the outer leaves die back. It is not an attractive look. In Massachusetts, I grew them in what would be described as high shade. There were no tree branches directly over the bed, but deciduous trees nearby would cast shadows over the garden during the heat of the summer. In Oregon, I have grown good looking plants in a bed with as little as half a day of sun, but I also grow some in full sun. The colors may be a bit brighter in the spring with more light, although those with silver, blue, or green leaves will look better with some shade. If you are having problems with a particular cultivar, you might want to try different light exposures before admitting defeat. Even the shade provided by a rock can be the difference between great growth and marginal growth.

In the southern US and other similar climates with long, warm, moist summers, some shade or protection is required. In Mississippi, I could only sustain them in raised planters (the soil was too rich and heavy) that I moved into the shade during the hot summer months. In these areas of the country, the high amounts of summer rain and humidity were an additional problem, and covering the planters with plastic to prevent too much rain exposure helped some. My best growth in Mississippi was in an area shaded by a roof, so that I could regulate water and light exposure. Keeping plants in portable containers is a better way than trying to use these directly in the garden in these extreme climates.

Moisture is the other major consideration, as I have alluded to previously. Some think of semps as cacti, which they are clearly not, even though they are succulent plants like cacti.

Semps are alpine plants, not plants of deserts. In the Alps, the plants would be covered in snow in winter, with little available water. Thus, in the winter here in temperate climates, with no or little snow cover, the plants are exposed to winter rain, for which they are not adapted. Cultivars with velvety or strongly cobwebbed rosettes often show damage in very wet winters. My friend Greg Colucci, who gardens in very winter wet Seattle, uses a plastic sheet to cover his beds of plants to eliminate the damaging effects of winter rain. Greg uses tubs like one would use for cattle feed to grow his plants, and this facilitates the ability to cover a fairly large collection. For those of us who use larger expanses of garden this becomes fairly impossible. I have used small clear plastic tops found on restaurant takeout boxes and placed them over especially susceptible cultivars. Be sure these containers are weighted down with rocks or fastened to the ground with landscape pins and raised sufficiently above the rosettes to insure some air circulation. Other people have used panes of glass raised above the clump of semps. Plan B is to simply avoid these difficult-to-grow cultivars. Most of the varieties described in "satin" categories in the cultivar list are predominantly *S. tectorum* blood, and these do the best in winter wet conditions. In contrast, in the summer months, I find that semp plantings do best when given one-half to one inch of water every week. This is what I do in Oregon, where summer rains are rather rare.

Planting is another concern. When plants are received from a mail-order nursery they are normally bare-rooted and quite dry. Polly Bishop had a habit of removing the rosettes from their bags and soaking the roots in a small volume of water so the plants could rehydrate from their trip; it does seem to allow the plants to respond more quickly. For the planting, make a shallow hole in your proposed planting site. Holding the rosette above the hole, fan out the roots so that they are spread throughout the hole. Gently fill in the soil in the hole and position the rosette so that it rests on top of the soil. Do not plant the rosette too deeply, thinking you are protecting it—you are only inviting rot! Many plants will arrive where the outermost leaves have reflexed a bit while in transit from the nursery. If they are extremely reflexed, it might be wise to remove a couple of the most reflexed leaves and plant the rosette as flatly as possible. The rosette shape will become more normal in time. After planting, water the plant with a transplanting fertilizer, such as Quick Start®, and cover the plant with an inverted berry basket or other cover for a few days until the plant is able to adjust to its new conditions. I find that spring plantings are best, as the weather is cooler and more consistently moist. Fall planting is next best, but it must be early fall, as the rosettes must grow new roots and establish before winter sets in, especially in colder regions.

An alternate planting technique is to grow the plants in pots first before subjecting them to the garden. Rare specimens and plants obtained from Europe that have been in transit for a long time are very dry and need to remake all of their roots. Take a good commercial, sterile potting mix and get it moist but not sopping and fill eight inch pots. If the plants have no roots, simply press the plants gently on top of the potting mix, give the pots a watering with a transplant fertilizer, and keep the pot in subdued light (a patio or the north side of the house) until new roots are formed. Monitor the pots closely, keeping them moist but not soupy, and keeping the plants free of dead leaves. After new roots form and growth of the rosettes is observed, the plants may be exposed to more light and eventually transplanted to the garden situation.

Mulching will help your plants in several ways. A fine grit (sometimes sold as chick grit) can be obtained at many farm stores and is an ideal size for mature rosettes. Smaller mixes of gravel with different colors can also be used that set off various colored rosettes a bit better than the more monochromatic chicken grit. Regardless of the type of grit, it performs two functions that help the survival of your plants. Like all mulches, grit will suppress the growth of weeds, which can be devastating to a semp planting. The grit also serves another function in curbing the splashing of soil during heavy rains on to the rosettes, which can induce rotting. The formation of new rosettes also seems to be better, in that the grit provides a perfectly dry start for the newly emerging rosette. The roots are still able to grow through the grit layer to obtain water.

Fig. 2-2. A semp bed mulched with fine gravel.

Planting distance is determined by what sort of effect you want to make, and also the size and methods of offset production. Large rosettes should be placed at least twelve to eighteen inches from each other, as they will quickly form large clumps and will start to intermingle in just a short time. Smaller rosettes can be planted proportionately closer. If a more immediate garden effect is required, a closer planting distance will give a nearly immediate ground cover. It is a good idea to put rosettes of contrasting form and color adjacent to each other so that the plants may be readily distinguished if they do begin to merge. The *heuffelii* cultivars make very compact clumps, and even though these are larger rosettes, can be planted near each other. The roller sorts should not be planted next to each other, but rather encircled by non-rollers, as the tiny offsets will travel rather large distances. If planted next to other rollers, the plants will be hopelessly mixed. In Lynn Smith's garden, she plants most of her roller types in the cavities of cement blocks to keep them more contained.

Because semps are smaller plants and will take abuse, they are ideal for areas in which a bed is too small for most plants but would look good with some sort of plantings. Areas near garages and along sidewalks and curbs are all prime sites for a semp planting. I have seen a number of such plantings that turn an eyesore into a bed with lots of interest. As I am writing this I am thinking I need to be listening to myself, as I have an area near my garage that could definitely use a nice bed of semps.

Labeling of the plants is a controversial matter. To those of us concerned with correct names on cultivars, permanent labels are a must. Labels should be proportionate to the size of the plant, or your planting may look more like a pet cemetery than a garden. I use a flag style label made of aluminum with a nice writing surface and a #2 pencil to write on the marker. These last many years, although the name of the plant is not easily discernible from a distance. Others affix computer generated labels to these that are easier to see. I use these labels on my bigger perennials, but not on the semps, because I am afraid of how they would look in a massed planting. Chris Rentmeister has produced very attractive acrylic markers with a dark background and white text. These are small and not garish. If you are more cavalier about labels, a chart of the planting with a clear mapping of the cultivars is next best. I generally also make a map of the planting, as it is amazing how labels can wander. I once had a child visiting my iris garden hand me a whole handful of labels that he had "thoughtfully" gathered for me. Luckily, the irises were still blooming, so moving the markers back to where they belonged was an easy matter. Doing this when they were out of flower would have been considerably more difficult!

ROCK GARDENS

What I have described so far are general techniques for growing semps, and also for creating semp-only or primarily semp gardens in raised beds. Although these can be landscape statements, one more often encounters semps in mixed plantings with other perennials. Semps are a perfect choice for rock gardens, as they are in fact Alpine plants and complement the forms and flowers of other rock plants. Some of these other rock garden companions are now discussed.

Although the details for construction of a rock garden are beyond the scope of this book, an excellent book on the subject is one by Rex Murfitt (2005) that gives details on their construction, especially smaller ones suited for most gardeners on less than palatial estates. This book describes all aspects of construction, and best of all has a semp on the cover.

➤ **Fig. 2-3.** Part of the rock garden of Chris Hansen.

◄ **Fig. 2-4.** Tim Stoehr's faux stream planted with semps.

➤ ⋎ Fig. 2-5-6.
Examples of
Mark Brandhorst's
use of semps with
rock crevices.

Perhaps a few comments on the rock gardens from my childhood will give you some ideas. Each of these was a solution to three different sorts of sites/terrains.

On my folks' property in Massachusetts, the yard had several natural slopes. On one of these we created the look of a rock outcropping, with large planting areas for semps and sedums. We were lucky, in that in New England, native rocks are abundant and an attractive rock garden featuring the lovely banded gneiss was constructed, giving patches of grey and white rock throughout the planting. Because the slope was very steep, the rocks were arranged almost in terraces, so that there were flat areas where semps could be grown.

Pat Drown-Warner's folks' yard was nearly flat, so the soil level was raised to create a berm and rocks were arranged so that it appeared an outcropping was just coming out of the ground. Semps were planted in the spaces between the rocks and the whole bed was raised above the level of the lawn. Soon the colonies formed a solid planting. It looked like a patchwork of different colors among the gray and white native banded gneiss used as the rock.

Polly Bishop had an unusual problem. Her driveway was a large (too hundred foot long) oval that separated a portion of lawn. A further problem was that the entire area was depressed in the center so it could form a pond. To create a garden, she scooped out paths that would become edges to each bed and then put in unmortared stone walls to keep the soil from rushing into the paths. Drains were installed so that the paths would not flood. Semps were planted all along the rocks, and in time huge clumps of semps spilled between the rocks. When Polly was constructing the garden, an extension of Route 2 was being constructed through my hometown. Several large ledges of rock were blasted to make the road cuts, providing all sorts of interesting rocks. The banded gneiss ledges gave rocks with predominantly white, pinkish, gray, banded, and shiny mica-enriched stones. Polly used slightly different rocks in the walls of each bed, and used complementary colored semps and other companion plants to feature these differences. Taller plants were planted in the middle of each bed to give some height, and also to set off the rock plants.

Thus, just in a mile's distance of the road, three very different sorts of terrains and three different solutions to creating rock gardens were made that would feature semps.

I should also include one planting in my present garden in Oregon, in what I term a "landscaping salvage" when I bought my house. When you buy a house, you also unfortunately buy the previous owner's landscape mistakes. I had a doozy of a mistake right next to my patio. The previous owner had installed a strange-sloped, raised bed in cement pavers with a faux stream (and water) running through the middle of it to a formal, three-tiered fountain. I am certainly no landscaper, but I do know to never mix formal and natural elements. The pool that contained the fountain was filled almost to the brim with soil and planted with water-loving irises (one of my other passions), while the outside of the strange cement structure was surrounded by a mass planting of daylilies to obscure the cement pavers, and the faux stream area was converted into a rock planting, with semps in the flatter areas and sedums flowing down the slope. It

is far from perfect, but certainly much less hideous. Although tearing it all out might have been the best solution, I am growing fonder of this area. It does take a bit to think of these diverse plants in juxtaposition, though.

If you are lucky enough to have property with a natural rock outcropping, you can readily dress this area up with the addition of semps. Make sure that the semps have sufficient soil to grow, and that soil from areas of the bed higher on the slope will not inundate the planting. Roller types will grow on areas with almost no soil. Place small rosettes in crevices and depressions in the rock and stand back. On the edge of my folks' property, one large rock protruded from the landscape and a crevice had developed that was filled with forest humus. Semps planted into the crevice quickly filled the crevice and looked natural there. In Maine, my friend Mark Brandhorst has used natural outcroppings to especially good effect, with the semps looking much as they would in the Alps.

I primarily use semps in most of my plantings, in relatively formal rectangular beds. Although these beds look good, a bit more imagination in a planting can make artistic statements. My friend Tim Stoehr planted a bed, but instead of a straight line, he fashioned a faux stream outlined by rocks with a gravel bed in which the semps were planted. This achieves not only a lovely garden statement, but also provides an ideal environment in which to grow semps.

For the last several years, our garden show of the Pacific Northwest, *Garden Time TV*, has come to my garden to shoot segments on exciting things in my yard. The semps were one of the topics. Judy and William, the hosts of the show, were impressed with the individual semps, but they were even more excited by the use of semps as ground covers. In a year's time, my seedling beds had formed a solid mat of colored rosettes. I had never thought of using them in such a role, but they would be ideal in situations where a larger, taller plant might look overpowering. I think we all have those sorts of odd corners in our yard: that bit of bare ground near the garage, at the edge of the patio, or near a garden shed. All could be transformed from eyesores into pretty plantings of semps.

In 1975, I was traveling on a concert tour and stayed in a marvelous resort in the Transylvanian Alps. This was the first time I had seen semps in the wild, but what impressed me most was the way the head gardener at one of the resorts had used semps. In a large, slightly sloped bed, he planted semps which had spelled out the month, day, and year using semps to create the letters and numbers! The arrangement was changed early each morning, although months and the year would of course be changed much less frequently. Very cool, I thought, and I have not seen it done since.

PLANTING IN CONTAINERS

Container gardening is a booming industry. Many people want to have plants, but have neither the time nor space to do a formal garden or rock garden. For those of us who are artistic or enjoy whimsy, semps are ideal, as they will work in so many types of containers. As you can see from the photos provided, we have a number of very creative gardeners using semps. I guess my New England upbringing (those darn Puritans!) makes me less willing to do this myself, but I can appreciate when others do it. In Mississippi, where conditions for growing semps were more difficult, I used stone troughs and whiskey barrels filled with a light potting soil. Because of the hot and humid conditions, these planters were always in shade in the summer and moved under the eaves to protect the plants from excess moisture in the winter. These portable gardens are a solution to growing semps in less favorable climates. My friend Bev Richards is a true artist in seeing potential planters in all sorts of would-be pots. By adding screening and peat strips to retain the soil, she has taken some very unorthodox structures and made clever semp planters out of them. Because of the very symmetrical nature of the semp rosette, they are especially useful in very geometric designs, but can also soften sharp edges by allowing the rosettes and offsets to cascade from the planter. As a

◄ ▲ Fig 2-8/
2-9. Examples of
Bev Richards's
work with unusual
planters.

▲ **Fig. 2-10.** A tufa planter created by Arthur and Janis Noyes featuring 'Pacific Joyce.'

◀ **Fig. 2-11.** A traditional planting of semps in a discarded boot.

youth, I saw many people growing semps in discarded boots and shoes. I found that odd as a kid, but now realize what better use for a frugal Yankee who could not stand the thought of throwing away a favorite shoe, but converted it into a planter adorned with semps.

One of the coolest uses of semps in containers was by one of our local suppliers of semps here in Oregon, Little Prince. The letters spelling out the name of their nursery were made up of pots of semps placed on their sides. This not only announced the name of the nursery, but was also a clever way to use plants. Really very clever marketing.

Many collectors also plant their collection in pots; this seems to be more the case in Europe, where collections are most often grown in pots. There are advantages to this system. Because pots are smaller and portable, one can grow more cultivars in a smaller space without fear of one cultivar growing into another. Soil and moisture conditions can be controlled exactly, and the

Fig. 2-12. A unique use of semps at Little Prince Nursery in Oregon.

pots may be lifted for close examination (better for aging gardeners who can't view semps planted in the ground). Plastic and clay pots have been used for semps with success. Clay is more breathable, but might require more watering. Howard Wills (Wills and Wills, 2004) has a system for growing his potted collection on cement risers that elevate a concrete slab several feet above the ground. The construction is pleasant looking and the plants are much closer to eye level. Pots can also be moved into shadier conditions if you garden in a climate in which summer conditions are too dry or humid and wet. Although plants exposed to full sun in these conditions might perish, those could be moved to shade. For growers concerned with correct identification of their cultivars, labeling is critical. In pots a label may be buried in the pot, etched into the pot lip, or as a more prominent label visible to the gardener.

Hypertufa is a man-made concoction that resembles the naturally occurring tufa, a lightweight rock that found favor with early rock gardeners to grow semps and other rock plants (Murfitt 2005). Although hypertufa resembles stone, it is much lighter, as it is composed of peat (and in some recipes perlite). The recipes are fairly simple, and containers may be made in very simple molds. Semps thrive in these pots, and a group of these containers can contain quite a large collection. Best yet, they are cheap to construct and much less expensive than stone planters.

Fig. 2-14. Beatrix Bodmeier's wonderful semp collection guarded by a gnome!

Soil in containers seems to be all over the place in terms of what works. Mixtures recommended by Peter Mitchell are variations on the famous John Innes composts. Wills and Wills (2004) gives a simple mix of fifty percent multipurpose compost (peat or peat-substitute based), twenty-five percent loam, and twenty-five percent coarse grit, the latter to ensure good drainage. As for plants grown in beds, semps look best and grow best when given a bit of gravel mulch. This prevents splash-up of soil on to the rosettes and helps the soil retain moisture. Because plants in pots require more constant attention as to water, this mulch is especially important. If the planter is fairly deep, one way to use less soil and also provide some drainage is to put a layer of packing peanuts at the bottom of the container and then put the potting medium over top. People have used clay and plastic pots, and there are merits and problems with each. Putting the pots into a gravel base and burying the pots in the gravel will help conserve moisture and keep the plants happy. These can be clustered in an area to facilitate watering and fertilizing regimes. Moreover, this will turn the collection of pots into an integrated planting more resembling a garden.

One of the most beautiful uses of semps I have ever seen were the huge driftwood sculptures in Winnie Crane's garden in Dalton, Massachusetts. With her head gardener Carlton Deame, Winnie came up with a most unusual sculpture garden using tall (up to six feet) pieces of driftwood that were transformed into living works of art with semps. Either natural crevices in the driftwood or holes cut into the driftwood with woodworking tools were filled with Milorganite® (an enriched compost made from sewage waste treatment in Milwaukee, Wisconsin) and thoroughly moistened, creating little pots of soil along the driftwood. Various sized semps were deposited in each of the holes. After several years, the semps had not only filled the cavities in the driftwood, but also spilled over into the surrounding areas of driftwood. To enhance the effect further, the driftwood was staged on a base of gravel and each was given a space, much like a sculpture garden, and surrounded by an area of gravel. The whole area was enclosed by a tall evergreen hedge with a narrow entrance, giving the effect of walking into a museum room. Not all of us have the resources or space to pull off such a grand scheme, but it does give us ideas to use a similar sort of planting with much smaller pieces of driftwood. My neighbor in Massachusetts, Polly Bishop, collected numerous smaller pieces of driftwood, looking for pieces with good cavities or interesting shapes to become semp planters. These were staged throughout the yard, sometimes covering up where a plant had winter killed or as an accent in sunken garden paths.

Cynda Foster, owner of Perennial Obsessions in Oregon, is truly an artist at using semps. My favorite of her creations are wreaths where semps and sedums are grown on the surface of a wreath-shaped growing structure. Within several months, the rosettes have grown into an impressive coverage of the structure. This living wreath lasts much longer than traditional evergreen wreaths and is not as seasonal; they look good year round. In addition, she has taken pots and other odd pieces and filled them with semps and other succulents that create year-round interest and are portable, so that any area may be decorated.

◄ ∧ Fig. 2-14 and 2-15.
Container plantings made by
Cynda Foster.

ROOF GARDENS

Semps are the original roof garden plant. S. *tectorum* was planted on roofs since ancient times as a charm against lightning. These are thatched roofs in most cases, and perhaps the semps also provided a bit of water repellency. Helen Payne (1972) simply threw extra bits of semps and sedums that were not used in her plantings up on a roof of one of her garden sheds. Within several years, the roof was a carpet of plants. Now this is Oregon, where rain is a bit more plentiful and temperatures are not as extreme. I am also betting that the shed roof had a good bit of moss and dead leaves that accumulated that served as a substrate upon which the plants could grow. A photo of the shed roof is published in Helen's book, and this was also a postcard that Helen would often enclose with her packages of relatively large orders.

Today, roof gardens are very popular, especially in industrial areas where a large flat roof is covered in soil and planted with a variety of succulents. Most of the succulents you see on roofs are sedums, and some commercial firms even sell prepackaged "lawns" of rooted sedum cuttings for this purpose. Semps are also used, but more occasionally. This sort of endeavor should not be undertaken by most of us. I would suggest attempting Helen's more casual approach for starting a green roof. Making the more sophisticated green roofs of today requires a highly qualified engineer and a construction team.

COMPANION PLANTS

Man (at least *this* man) does not live on semps alone! There are so many other neat plants out there, and many of these will augment the look of semps in a garden setting. Almost all of the plants that rock gardeners choose are excellent companions to semps, as are many other succulent plants. There are several rules for companion plants for semps:

1) The companion plant must not be so vigorous or large that it invades the semp clump and grows through it.

2) The companion plant should be small enough that the semps are not shaded by the mass of the plant, affecting their growth.

3) The companion plant should require similar sorts of soil and water requirements as the semps so that watering and fertilizing will not adversely affect either the companion plant or the semps.

Luckily, we have lots of good choices that fulfill these criteria. I am an unabashed lover of irises and have been breeding them nearly as long as I have semps (see Vaughn 2015). In my garden I have several raised beds of dwarf and median irises that are edged with clumps of semps. Occasionally the semp or the iris will grow into each other, but because both plants are easy to transplant this is a minor inconvenience at best. The colors and patterns of dwarf and median irises are almost limitless. Plants range in height from three to twenty-seven inches tall, and by judicious choices of cultivars several months of bloom can be obtained. Reblooming cultivars will give even longer bloom. Bearded irises go dormant in the summer and will want less moisture then, although I do give the irises water at least once a week during very dry Oregon summers. The semps seem to appreciate this too.

Small bulbs, especially spring ephemeral bulbs, such as some of the miniature and small daffodils, are also excellent companions to semps. The bigger sorts of daffodils have larger foliage that, when it senesces, could fall over the semps and cause rotting problems. The golden color of many of these small and miniature daffodils are beautiful when contrasted with dark red or purple semp rosettes.

In California and parts of the desert southwestern US, numerous yards use cactus and succulent gardens to create xeric gardens that are beautiful landscape statements. Semps of course would prefer colder climates than this, but it may be possible to create similar effects by using a different pallet of succulent plants (Chance 2016). Taller accent plants, such as yucca, agave, or hardy cactus, can give height to the bed which is lacking in most cold hardy succulents.

Succulent cousins of the semps *Sedum*, *Orystachys*, and *Rosularia* are all excellent companions to semps and add lots of interest to a planting with their varying but complementary forms and colors. Some sedums may be too vigorous or sprawling to put in close company with semps. Luckily sedum breeders Brent Horvath and Chris Hansen have produced a series of sedum hybrids that are good low-growing and clumping plants (Horvath 2014). I use these plants down the middle of primarily semp beds to add a bit of height and texture difference. Two of the best Western US sedums, *Sedum spathulifolium* and *S. laxum*, are both great companion plants for semps, making neat, slowly increasing clumps with a sea of yellow flowers over the clump in mid-summer. Many excellent clones of these species are available from specialist nurseries, with *Sedum spathulifolium* 'Cape Blanco' being a lovely silvery blue. Some of the saxifrages have a rosette shape like semps, but I find them to be a little too fussy as to their requirements even here in the gardening paradise of Oregon. However, if you have had luck with these plants, it is worth trying them as a contrast in semp beds. You might even fool a semp enthusiast as to, "what kind of strange semp is that?" If you do not mind "pushing your zone," there are all sorts of wonderful less hardy succulent plants. Aloes are especially attractive with semps. If planted in pots that are submerged in the beds, these can be lifted and brought indoors or in a greenhouse for the winter months.

If you wish to keep the bed as a succulent only garden but want flowers too, the *Delosperma* (ice plant) cultivars and species are an answer to your prayers; these are one of the jewels of the flora of South Africa. The flowers are sort of daisy-shaped and come in a variety of colors, including a bright orchid, apricot, yellow, white, and shades of pink on chunky plants with pretty pale green leaves, sometimes shaded purple. Bloom comes quickly and the plants spread rather quickly to make a nice carpet, but are easily contained. Lynn Smith has grown these cultivars here in wet winter Oregon and they survive even in the very cold winters of Colorado. Rooting of these plants is simple if you want to increase your planting. Bloom is virtually non-stop in Oregon.

Some of the smaller, hardy geraniums are lovely with semps. In my garden, the smaller varieties of *Geranium sanguineum*, with flowers in shades of white, pink, and magenta, are great garden companions to semps. The hardy geranium hybrid 'Joy' is an especially neat growing and restrained plant, with flowers of a soft lavender. The contrast of leaf textures of these hardy geraniums with the semp rosettes is an especially effective garden combination. Similarly, small cultivars of *Dianthus* form neat mounds of often silver foliage. Flowers come in all shades of pink, red, and white, with varying types and levels of red or pink markings. Avoid *Dianthus delltoides* though, as it is too rampant a spreader to be a good companion plant to your semps. The stars of western US flora are the penstemon species, especially the small "shrubby types" such as *Penstemon rupicola* and other related species and hybrids (Lindgren and Wilde 2003); these are excellent mixed with semps. Although these are called shrubs, they are really more like other herbaceous perennials, and their tidy clumps of evergreen foliage look good year round. Best yet, they like exactly the same conditions as semps.

Plants to avoid planting with semps are anything that seeds about too readily. I love the alliums, but many of these have a nasty habit of seedling about, often right in the middle of the semp clump—not good. There are also a lot of other "garden thugs" that will grow right over semps. Some of the faster growing sedums, creeping phlox, and vinca are three that are best left out of semp beds. All of these will quickly cover semps. In the wild, semps grow in many places that would be inhospitable to competing plants, but in the garden situation these more rapidly growing plants will have the upper hand.

YEARLY CALENDAR OF SEMP CULTURE

Semps are sometimes ignored in the garden because they are so relatively carefree. To obtain optimal results, a few general rules for growing semps will help your enjoyment with these plants and impress others as to their beauty. Below is a brief summary of the tasks to be performed throughout the seasons:

Spring: This is an optimal time to purchase new cultivars for your garden. They will quickly root and be well-established by the time warmer summer temperatures occur. This is also the time of year that a little fertilizing will help the color and size of the rosettes. I use a simple transplant fertilizer that is relatively low in nitrogen so as not to make lush growth that might be prone to rot. Early in the spring, removing the dead leaves from the base of the rosette will improve the looks of your plants and may prevent rotting later in the season. If you are growing your collection in pots, transfer the rosettes to new soil and mulch the surface with gravel.

Summer: Here is a time you may need to water your semps, even those planted in beds and mulched with gravel. Do not overdo it even then. Touch the soil surface and see if it is dry. If so, give them a good soaking during the cool portions of the day. Never water when the temperature is above 80°F, or you will be inviting rot. If you are not saving the seed to grow on, you may clip out the blooming rosettes to improve the looks of the clumps and to prevent stray seedlings from contaminating your named cultivars. Be on the lookout for rot, and remove affected leaves or rosettes from your clumps. If extremely hot weather is predicted, there are a number of shade cloths that can be put over the beds to keep the plants cooler.

Fall: This is another time for tidying up your plants in anticipation of winter. Removing dead leaves that could rot in the winter is a good exercise to prevent these dead leaves from becoming places for more rot. Getting rid of all weeds in the beds will help with spring cleanup, and will lessen weed pressures in the future. If you live in a relatively benign climate, new plants may be obtained and established before winter cold sets in. Make sure all seed heads are removed before the seed has a chance to fall unless you are saving the seed.

Winter: If you live in a *very* wet climate, and especially if you have some of the more hairy species, some sort of protection is a good idea, especially for the more susceptible cultivars or species. Try to find protection that protects the plant from rain but not light. Glass panes, acrylic sheets, or covers from plastic vegetable store containers are all good. The lighter ones should be fastened down. Winter winds are *strong* and your protection might be in the next state if it is not fastened down/weighted. Weeding in the winter is something some of us in winter wet climates have to face, too. Weeds such as bittercress can quickly overcome a patch of ground, so be sure to check your plantings even in winter.

Although semps are easy garden subjects, growing them optimally will make for a much more beautiful plant and the pleasure you derive from these well-grown plants will be much more.

REFERENCES

Chance L (2016) "Pushing the limits: landscaping with cacti and succulents in cold climates." *Cactus & Succulent J* 88: 234–241

Correvon H (1929) *Les Joubarbes* (translated into English in 1975 by the Sempervivum Society and published by Southern Reprographics, Sussex UK)

Horvath B (2014) *The Plant Lover's Guide to Sedums*. Timber Press. Portland, Oregon

Lindgren D, E Wilde (2003) *Growing Penstemons: Species, Cultivars, and Hybrids*. Infinity Publishing. Haverford, PA

Murfitt R (2005) *Creating and Planting Alpine Gardens*. Mackey Books. Wayne, PA

Payne, H (1972) *Plant Jewels of the High Country, Sempervivums and Sedums*. Pine Cone Pub. Medford, OR

Raes P (2014) "To grow or not grow on limestone, that's the question." *Sedum Soc Newsletter* 110: 93-96

Vaughn KC (2015) *Beardless Irises, A Plant for Every Garden Situation*. Schiffer Publishing, Atglen, PA

Wills H, S Wills (2004) *An Introduction to Sempervivum and Jovibarba Species and Cultivars*. Fernwood Nursery, UK

CHAPTER 3

SEMPERVIVUM SPECIES

This is a book for gardeners, not for botanists. Although the species were important garden subjects when I started growing semps over fifty years ago, today they play a much less important role in terms of garden subjects. Many are undistinguished dirty green, or greens with purple tips. When I started growing semps again, I realized that most were now uninteresting garden subjects compared to the many hybrids. Many of these were semps that only a mother could love. Moreover, many, especially the species from Turkey and Iran, are rather touchy garden subjects, being sensitive to moisture and/or humidity. Because of this, my discussion of the species will be predominantly in several areas: the history of the taxonomy of this group of plants, what species forms are still fine garden subjects, and those species that have played a major role in the development of the hybrids.

R. LLOYD PRAEGER AND HIS ROLE IN DEFINING *SEMPERVIVUM* SPECIES

The taxonomic situation of the genus *Sempervivum* was in a terrible mess when Irish botanist R. Lloyd Praeger began investigating this group. Praeger summarized the situation: "It is doubtful if any genus of plants is in such a confused state in our gardens and our garden books." Previous to this time, botanists would visit the Alps, find an interesting specimen that differed from others, give it a species name, and add another "species" to an already cluttered group of "species." Unfortunately, these workers were not aware that semp species cross readily, and these hybrids can cross with each other and back to the parent species. Evidence of three species in a single natural hybrid have been documented. Praeger recognized this and sorted out much of it—especially the species from the Alps—into the true species and dismissed the many hybrids as just that. As he stated, "Among the European Sempervivums, the presence of unrecognized interspecific hybrids led to the description of 'species' before their true character was demonstrated, and the confusion still persists, especially in gardens." Almost all of the species that Praeger defined have stood the test of time. By observing many of these plants in the wild, he was much more able to make these assessments than botanists that relied on dubious specimens in botanical gardens or herbarium specimens. Succulents are poorly preserved using standard plant pressing techniques, so herbarium specimens are not as useful in semps as they are in other non-succulent plants. My copy of Praeger's monograph, *An Account of the Sempervivum Group* (1932), came as a graduation present from Polly Bishop and is still a treasured possession. Reprints of this classic work are now available so that others may read Praeger's words.

Praeger did not limit his interest to the semps. In his monograph, he also described the tender relatives of the semps, such as species of the genus *Aeonium*. In addition, he produced a similar classic monograph on sedums and also authored a number of other classic botanical works, including *Aspects of Plant Life* (1921), *The Way That I Went* (1937), and *The Botanist in Ireland* (1934). All of these are good reads and give you an idea of Praeger's love of all things botanical. I wish I had met this most interesting gentleman. World renowned sedum expert Ray Stephenson even suggested that if he could play the game of inviting anyone he wanted to have dinner, it would be Lloyd Praeger. I think Praeger would be on my short list, too.

POST PRAEGER

Several authors added to Praeger's taxonomic work, even though these people were not taxonomists per se. Alan Smith obtained the collection of Hugh Miller, which were the plants Praeger used in his studies. Alan sold these plants through his nursery and also authored a small booklet, *The Genus Sempervivum and Jovibarba* (1975), which described a lot of the plants and some of the more recent additions. Because of the distribution of the plants that had been verified by Praeger, we were on very firm ground as to the plants in our gardens matching the species described by Praeger. Peter Mitchell, organizer of the Sempervivum Society, was fascinated by the species and he wrote *The Sempervivum and Jovibarba Handbook* (1973). Basically this book updated Praeger's work to include the newly described species from Turkey and Iran. He also expressed the new view that *S. heuffelii* and the members of the *S. globiferum* complex should be classified under the genus *Jovibarba* based upon their floral anatomy and different mode of vegetative reproduction in that group. This was the accepted taxonomic status of the genus at the time of Mitchell's work.

The most recent thorough taxonomic treatment of the group is that of t' Hart et al. (2003), and is the taxonomy which is followed in this book. This taxonomic revision keeps *Sempervivum* as a single genus with sections *Sempervivum* and *Jovibarba*, the latter containing those species previously in *Jovibarba*. I thought that their description of the problems in defining species in the genus especially apropos:

> In general, *Sempervivum* species have proved difficult to define and the nomenclature is often complicated and/or confused. Quite often different authors have subsequently classified certain taxa as species, subspecies, varieties or even mere forms. In addition, opinions on relationships and the systematic position of many taxa sometimes diverge largely and on some occasions these differences have resulted in seemingly random shifts of certain infraspecific taxa from one species to another.

Thus, despite over eighty years since Praeger's monumental work, the taxonomic issues since then have still added much confusion. The synthesis of t'Hart et al. (2003) is a very rational examination of the taxonomy by several experts in the field and represents a good stabilization of the taxonomy of the group. Approximately fifty species of *Sempervivum* were discussed, although a few of these are only known from their type collections. More species are still being discovered in Iran and other areas of the Middle East and former Soviet Union. Because these are dangerous areas for exploration at present it is unlikely that these species will be clarified in the near future.

The taxonomic analysis of t'Hart et al. (2003) grouped the *Sempervivum* into a single genus, rather than dividing them into two genera, *Sempervivum* and *Jovibarba*. The rationale for this grouping is as follows:

1) The *Jovibarba* species are diploids with a base chromosome number that falls within the range of the remainder of the genus.

2) Hybrids may be obtained by crossing the *Jovibarba* species with members of the rest of the genus, although with difficulty.

3) Molecular studies indicate a close relationship between the two genera.

4) Morphologically, the two groups share more similarities than differences, e.g., all are immediately recognizable as semps.

For these reasons they denote two sections of the genus: section *Jovibarba*, containing *S. globiferum* and *S. heuffelii*, with the remaining species grouped in section *Sempervivum*.

Traditional taxonomy was done by botanists who were documenting characteristics of the leaves and flowers that distinguished them from other plants. However, traits that are obvious to us as extreme differences, like red rosette color or yellow flowers, may be due to only one or several genes. For example, a classification used in the book of Wills and Wills (2004) divided the species into two tribes: one with red flowers (section Rhodanthe) and one with yellow flowers (section Chrysanthae). Although this was a convenient way of grouping the species, it was an artificial system based on a single character, and actually separated species we now know are closely related. With the advent of molecular biology, we can now use DNA analysis to much more accurately determine relationships between species and also determine the phylogeny of the group. Cladistic analysis—using computer programs—groups the organisms based on similarity of their DNA sequences into classes called clades. These DNA studies are less biased, and they are analyzed in computer programs that establish the groups, not arbitrary decisions based on morphology. Two studies have addressed these questions, trying to determine which groups within the Crassulaceae gave rise to the genus (Mort et al. 2001) and to determine how the species are related to each other (Klein and Kadereit 2015).

In the study by Mort et al. (2001), a number of the species of the Crassulaceae were probed with three chloroplast DNA markers. Chloroplast DNA is inherited maternally, much like mitochondrial DNA in humans, and thus has the added advantage of determining the maternal parent in given lines of evolution. When these genes were examined, the genus *Sempervivum* appears to have arisen out of a group that includes *Sedum rupestre*. In their study, the species in the *Sempervivum* and *Jovibarba* sections appear as a single clade, although the species in the *Jovibarba* and *Sempervivum* sections do resolve as separate. Most interestingly, the tender genera from the Canary Islands, such as *Aeonium*, *Aichryson*, *Greenovia*, and *Monanthes*, are in fact *not* related closely to the semps, even though many authors, including Praeger, considered them to be closely related based on morphology of the plants. Mort et al. (2001) only examined eight species of *Sempervivum*, and they showed such close relationships that separating the species from each other or showing relationships between them and reconciling them was not possible using these probes.

Klein and Kadereit (2015) examined a much greater number of species and accessions, including almost all the species we now recognize, and used a variety of nuclear and chloroplast DNA probes in their analysis. In these studies, all of the rollers and *S. heuffelii* came out as a group which is sister to all of the other semps. Within the *Jovibarba* sub-genus, *S. heuffeili* came out as a sister group to all the roller types. Within the other *Sempervivum*, there were clades that included certain species based on similarities in nuclear DNA, although these clades were often not supported by the chloroplast DNA data. Some of the data support previous groupings of the species, such as *S. calcareum* and *S. tectorum* being more closely related and the species from Turkey and Iran being related. Because the mutation rate of DNA can be calculated, these authors were able to estimate that the *Jovibarba* and *Sempervivum* sections of the genus separated about five to nine million years ago, and that most of the intra-sub-genus diversification took place within the past two million years. Thus, the genus *Sempervivum* is a relatively young one and still in the process of diversification. This explains in part why the species are so able to cross with each other, as they have only been separated for such a short time and compatibility still exists. Certainly there are few other genera in which virtually all of the species have been crossed with each other and where many of these hybrids are also fertile.

CYTOLOGICAL STUDIES

The chromosomes of *Sempervivum* species are tiny in comparison with other species, and even experienced scientists have trouble producing good chromosome squashes. The work of Charles Uhl is considered among the most definitive, as he was an expert at getting good chromosome squashes of these notoriously difficult members of the Crassulaceae. A summary of all of these cytological studies is listed on the Sempervivophili website (see appendix). The basic chromosome number of the *Sempervivum* ranges from 16–21, with the species in the *Jovibarba* section only at 19, and these species are all diploids. Within the *Sempervivum* section, diploids (with two sets of chromosomes) and tetraploids (four sets of chromosomes) are both known, sometimes with diploid and tetraploid forms of a single species, such as in *S. arachnoideum*. Hybrids between the tetraploid and diploid species produce triploids (three sets of chromosomes) with more limited fertility, whereas crosses between tetraploid forms form amphidiploid hybrids (hybrids with diploid genomes of both parental species) with high levels of fertility. Because so many of the semp species have high chromosome numbers, a quantity of the species appear to be ancient tetraploids or amphidiploids. Certainly, the segregation of characters in the hybrids is indicative of tetraploid segregations of many characters. Only in S. *heuffelii* does one see good simple Mendelian segregations of characters, such as rosette colors and leaf patterns. As a rule of thumb, species with chromosome counts of 32–42 are diploid plants, whereas species with 48 and more chromosomes are tetraploids or amphidiploids. This general rule will help you in your hybridizing to produce the most fertile hybrids.

THE "BIG FIVE" ALPINE SPECIES

The Alps is the center of diversity of the genus, and in this area five species are found that make up not only the majority of collected forms, but natural and man-made hybrids account for a majority of the semps in terms of their ancestry. This has been a great boon to us hybridizing semps, as these species are morphologically and genetically diverse, creating a rich pallet of genes for further hybridization. Each of these species has contributed unique qualities to the hybrids, and most of these species are fairly easy garden subjects, even far from their Alpine homes.

S. tectorum

When a non-semp person says "I have the green one," this is generally the plant they have. S. *tectorum* is the largest species (up to eight inches), and also one of the most diverse. Although the most commonly grown form of this species is a green with prominent purple leaf tips, other forms are flushed with red or violet, suffused with red at the leaf bases, and even forms without the very characteristic purple tip. The clone presently being distributed as 'Isabela' is close to the common form from the rooftops in Europe. Size also varies tremendously. The most commonly cultivated form has been grown for such a long time asexually from stolons that it has lost some of its ability to reproduce by sexual means, with its pollen often aborted and few if any seed found on it. Fortunately, other clones are fully fertile and S. *tectorum* is a prolific outcrossing species, giving rise to a series of hybrids with all the species with which it grows and virtually everything grown in gardens as well. Because S. *tectorum* is a tetraploid (chromosome count of 72), the progeny are often fertile, and crosses back to the parental species and among the hybrids have transferred the traits of *tectorum* to these hybrids. What *tectorum* contributes to its hybrids are large size, a greater toughness to changes in climate, and relatively smooth or even glaucous leaves. Selections in violet and with red bases have passed these valuable genes on to their progeny. Indeed, S. *tectorum* is the source of the very popular darker purples and red-green bicolors for the most part. These are certainly among the most desirable of all semp plants, and we owe their beauty to this variable and hardy species.

▶ **Fig. 3-1.** *S. tectorum*

◀ **Fig. 3-2.** *S. montanum* 'Cmiral's Yellow'

S. montanum

S. montanum is a smaller plant (two to three inches in diameter) than *S. tectorum*, but its distinguishing feature is the very velvety surface of the leaf. Flowers of this plant are quite pretty, sort of a pinkish blended with violet, and larger than most semps. Hybrids from *montanum* nearly always exhibit velvety leaves. The form known as 'Rubrum' was one of the chief sources of red color in the velvety red hybrids. The popular hybrid 'Cleveland Morgan' is probably a selection from that plant. *S. montanum* is generally a diploid of 42 chromosomes, although the *ssp. stiriacum* is a tetraploid of 84 chromosomes. This subspecies has prominent purple tips to the leaves and is sometimes given species status by some taxonomists. *S. montanum* grows at higher altitudes than other species, and it often confers great hardiness in its hybrids as well. With its velvety leaves, it can be a bit more sensitive to winter wet than other species. The cultivar 'Cmiral's Yellow' is a bright gold, but is a notorious poor grower.

S. wulfenii

S. wulfenii is not a good garden plant, as it is one of the poorest increasers of any semp, with rather thick stolons on the few offsets that are formed. It is also a very distinctive species, and it has added a number of interesting characters to the world of semps. In most of the clones of this species, the inner leaves are gathered into a conical bud and the leaves are broad and of a lovely glaucous blue green. Hybrids from this species have inherited some of these qualities. The popular velvety hybrids, such as 'Aymon Correvon' and 'Purdy's 90-1,' have the silver color indicative of a cross of S. montanum and S. wulfenii, as does their relative sterility, as S. wulfenii is a diploid with 36 chromosomes, so hybrids between the two would have at least 6 unpaired chromosomes. Similarly, hybrids such as 'Soul,' 'Silverine,' and 'Silver Song' exhibit some of the rosette shapes and silvery colors from S. wulfenii. Luckily, these hybrids are fertile, perhaps due to some S. tectorum heredity as well.

S. arachnoideum

Certainly one of the gems of the genus is this species: the "cobweb houseleek," so named because of the arrangement of hairs at the tip of each leaf that are connected to form a mass resembling a cobweb. One of my friends had convinced herself that the plant I sent her was not covered with a cobweb, but rather covered in fungus, and set about removing the offending "pathogen," trying to remove the cobweb from these plants. Be assured, this is no fungus. The cobweb is not constant throughout the season, but rather, seems to be at its height in the summer, with a reduced amount of cobwebbing in the winter. This seasonal shift may indicate some of the roles of the cobweb: a protection from the sun during the summer, and also possibly absorbing the morning dew as a water source, much as some epiphytic plants use similar structures. In the wild, there are even some forms of S. arachnoideum with no cobweb, or only a vestigial one.

All S. arachnoideum cultivars are small, with some of these extreme size forms, sometimes giving subspecies status. The subspecies tomentosum is recognized by t' Hart et al. (2003) as the larger, very heavily cobwebbed form. This subspecies is always tetraploid, so it is one to use in crosses for the most fertile offspring, even in crosses to other species. The subspecies known as bryoides tends to be the smallest one, its names indicating a "moss-like" look. However, there is a complete gradation of sizes from the smallest to the largest, making it difficult to characterize any subspecies just upon size.

Although most semps have relatively undistinguished flowers, those of S. arachnoideum are a particularly fine bright rose flower of relatively large size on relatively short stalks. The contrast between the white cobweb and the bright rose flowers is a definite garden statement. S. arachnoideum is often the first species to bloom, with flowers even as early as late June and early July in Oregon. Besides, the normal rose-flowered form—a clone with white flowers—is also known, although for me, this has always been a very weak clone.

S. arachnoideum contributes all sorts of wonderful things to its hybrids. Although most of the seedlings do not have a full cobweb, most will have at least a tuft of hair on the tip of each leaf. These terminal hairs often give a frosted look to the rosette. Size is very affected in S. arachnoideum hybrids, as even crosses to the very large S. tectorum give hybrids not much bigger than S. arachnoideum. Flowers are also often better in these hybrids than those from other hybrid matings, often with a similar bright rose to that found in the species. S. arachnoideum marks its hybrids, but in most wonderful ways, and its hybrids are some of the most popular of all semps. Most of the arachnoideum clones have a good deal of red color, some quite intense, and this characteristic is also found in a number of the hybrids.

S. grandiflorum

Like S. montanum, S. grandiflorum is a velvety green species, but there the similarity ends. Whereas S. montanum has more compact rosettes with broader leaves, S. grandiflorum has rather open rosettes with long, tapered, almost pointed leaves. As one might expect from the name, the flowers of S. grandiflorum are larger than most (roughly two inches in diameter) and a yellow sort of tinged greenish, again distinct from the red flowers of S. montanum. The leaves feel sort of sticky, no doubt due to the large number of resin-containing trichomes, which also give this species its distinctive and not good—at least to me—smell.

Although S. grandiflorum does cross readily with the other alpine species, it seems to have less impact on present day hybrids than the other Alpine species. It is a tetraploid with a chromosome count of 80, so should be able to make fertile hybrids with the other species. The hybrid 'Yvette' is perhaps closest to the species itself, and it is a wonderful garden plant, forming a neat carpet of velvety green leaves with a distinct and precise purple tip. 'Yvette' has done very well in my garden and is a nice touch of the S. grandiflorum look.

Fig. 3-3. 'Yvette'

SPECIES OF THE *JOVIBARBA* SECTION

The species in the *Jovibarba* section are characterized by flowers that have a campanulate form (literally like a bellflower, *Campanula*) in shades of lemon, and more rarely near white. There are two very distinct species in this section with totally opposite mechanisms of rosette division.

S. heuffelii

S. heuffelii may be my favorite semp. It makes tidy clumps of rosettes that divide by crown splitting rather than by offsetting, and the rosettes are very sturdy, looking good throughout the year. The bloomstalks are rather frequent, at least in Oregon, and have blooms of a good yellow. In cultivars with red rosettes the flower stalk leaves are also red, and these contrast with yellow flowers, making a lovely effect. Best yet, because of the tight nature of the clump, the blooms make no annoying gap in the clump. Just about a perfect plant. The type of the species was the hairy form of the species—more rare than the glabrous form, which seems an odd choice for a taxonomist to have made. Most of the cultivars are also of the glabrous type. When I first started growing semps in the '60s, there were very few cultivars available in the US and few people were breeding them. This changed when Ed Skrocki and Bill Nixon began growing seedlings from the better forms, and suddenly more unusual colors started to appear among the seedlings. The Europeans have taken up the slack since and now several thousand selections are available. Forms are available from yellow, orange, palest green, pink, shades of violet, reds from maroon and cherry to deep red, and colors approaching true browns and near blacks. Many of my favorites are listed

52

Fig. 3-4. A wild *S. heuffelii*

in the recommended cultivars section of this book. When Bill Nixon was forced to reduce his collection this species was the last to go, as a measure of his respect for this species. If you are the kind of gardener that wants to plant something and forget it, this species is for you. The clump never needs to be dug and divided unless you want to.

There are also hybrids of *S. heuffelii* with the rollers to produce the hybrid known as *S. x nixonii* (honoring semp enthusiast Bill Nixon). Although these are of academic interest in that they can be created, I really prefer the pure *S. heuffelii* forms in most instances. 'Jowan' to me is the nicest of the hybrid forms, looking like a more narrow and pointed leaf of *S. heufellii*. I have obtained very few seeds from these hybrids when the stalks were left to be open pollinated; I have never obtained any progeny.

S. globiferum

The so-called "rollers" are all cultivars/clones of this one species. Formerly, this species was actually four species, but are now subspecies of *S. globiferum*. The four subspecies differ in size, shape of the rosette, and shape of the leaves in the rosette. All produce their offsets on very weak stolons, so unlike the majority of semps that are linked to the mother rosette by a rather stout stolon, the offsets tend to detach rapidly, with the offsets falling around the mother rosette. This species is probably responsible for the nickname "hens-and-chickens," as it does appear to be a mother hen rosette with a bunch of tiny chicks all about. Because the daughter rosettes do roll, it is a good plan to somehow compartmentalize the area around these plants, either by growing non-roller cultivars surrounding the roller cultivar or providing a physical barrier. Greg Colucci constructs small rock barriers to arrest the rolling

of the offsets. My friend Lynn Smith cleverly uses the cavities in cement building blocks filled with soil to grow her roller types. The ridge of the cavity keeps the rollers neatly in place with no worries. Very clever, as they can be a challenge to keep in place. They are very cool plants and worth the effort. They are also almost foolproof plants. If you have trouble growing semps then these might be the ones to try.

S. globiferum ssp. allioni is generally a paler plant than the other subspecies and quite small (roughly one to 1½ in.). It makes very neat small clumps and is a bit less productive of an offset producer than some of the other subspecies, and has more hair than the other subspecies. Many of the collected forms that have been cultivated are a greenish yellow. *S. globiferum ssp. arenaria* is a very small rosette with a many-leaved form, like little green buttons. This subspecies very rarely blooms in cultivation. *S. globiferum ssp. globiferum* is the most common type, and is often found under the name *soboliferum*. It is a bigger plant than the first two subspecies and taller, with incurved leaves. *S. globiferum ssp. hirtum* is a most distinctive plant. Unlike the other species that have more incurved leaves, *hirtum* has very open, almost stellate rosettes that do not incurve. Some selections of *hirtum* will get up to three to four inches in diameter and are often boldly marked with red or purple tips.

Unlike many other semps, the hybrids in the roller types are rather rare, and most of the cultivars available are selections from the wild, rather than the work of deliberate or even accidental hybridizing. A few of these cultivars are mentioned in the cultivar section of this book. The most interesting ones have extra bits of red, or are pale gold to yellow.

OTHER GOOD SPECIES FOR THE GARDEN

Although I started out this chapter by disparaging the species a bit, there are some species that have yet to be surpassed in our garden hybrids. Most of these are fairly easy garden plants.

S. calcareum

In some respects, *S. calcareum* resembles *S. tectorum* in its green leaves with distinct purple tips, but the rosettes are much more compact in form and generally have a hint of blue or glaucous waxiness to enhance the color (Dumont and Dumont 2013). As the name would indicate, this species prefers to grow on calcareous (limestone) soil/rock in the wild, but in gardens, it is much more forgiving of such conditions, and in my garden it seems easily adaptable to the acidic soil conditions of my Massachusetts and Oregon gardens. Unlike many species, *S. calcareum* is much less inclined to flower under garden conditions here in the US and soon forms neat clumps of rosettes. Indeed, Helen Payne questioned me on the pedigree of my 'Greenwich Time' ('Cleveland Morgan' X *S. calcareum*), as she had never seen this species bloom. Several years later, a box arrived with a blooming rosette of this species and a card saying, "I believe you now." Blooms seem to be most frequent in years when the summer temperatures are high. This year in Oregon we had unprecedented heat, and all but one of my *S. calcareum* clones bloomed. The flowers of this species are rather distinctive—a cream with pink bases—and the bloomstalk is rather short, so it is one of the species for which the blooms complement the attractiveness of the clump, rather than detract.

Clumps of *S. calcareum* spread out nicely, and unlike many, do not require frequent divisions to maintain an attractive look. One negative of this species is the rigidity of the leaves. Although this is a virtue in some respects, the senescing leaves do not senesce like other species, leaving grey "leaf skeletons" at the periphery of the rosette. If these leaves are removed once or twice in the season then the looks of the clumps are retained. Otherwise, a very easy species to grow and a most beautiful one.

When I was a child, there was but a single cultivar available here in the US. Now, we have a large number of wild accessions and cultivars of garden origin available for the gardener. There are no bad ones in this group. My favorite of the green with purple tips is 'Extra.' All of the *calcareum* cultivars are very symmetrical, but this one seems especially so, with very neat spirals of leaves and each one perfectly tipped. 'Extra' is a bit bigger than some of the other cultivars too. If you can't find 'Extra,' 'Sir William Lawrence' is a good choice in similar colors. 'Limelight' is a very pale lime green with no deeper tip. This lack of anthocyanin pigment results in an exceptionally clean and refreshing color. The clone of *S. calcareum* from Ceuse is similar and may be a bit better grower. Unlike many pale cultivars, this is one that has no problems growing. Planted next to dark semps seems to enhance this pale color. 'Pink Pearl'—a collected form—has lovely pinkish tips to the leaves and a little flush to the leaf bases, giving a quite different effect than the purple-tipped forms. 'Grigg's Surprise' (also known as *S. calcareum* 'Monstrosum') is a very special cultivar. The leaves of this cultivar are folded back upon themselves, so instead of forming a flat lamina, a tube-like leaf is produced. The tip of this tube is marked with the same dark purple as in the species. Even the petals of the flowers produce this same rolled phenotype. This plant was so unique that taxonomists did not even recognize it as a semp! Rumors were this plant had come from Iran (then Persia) and it was named *'Cotyledon persicum.'*

Hybrids from *calcareum* are rare, and it seems even in nature it rarely hybridizes with other species. It has been presumed, based on chromosome constitution, that *S. tectorum* is an ancient natural amphidiploid hybrid of *S. calcareum* and perhaps *S. marmoreum*. The sparse bloom and its diploid constitution may be other factors that have discouraged the production of hybrids from this plant both in the wild and in cultivation.

S. cantabricum

This species has been a most pleasant surprise since my move to Oregon in 2010, as it was not generally available in the US when I was breeding semps as a child. It is still rarely offered by nurseries but is worth seeking out. The rosettes are basically medium sized and bright green with slightly incurved form and varying amounts of purple at the leaf tip depending on the subspecies. Mark Smith (1981) did a very thorough description of these subspecies. *S. cantabricum ssp. cantabricum* is densely hairy, an incurved rosette, and pigmented tips greater than two millimeters. *S. cantabricum ssp. guadarrannense* is much less hairy, less incurved than *cantabricum*, and has a pigmented leaf tip greater than two millimeters. *S. cantabricum ssp. urbionense* is smaller than the other subspecies, densely hairy, and with very little anthocyanin at the leaf tip. All are fine plants. In my garden, the bloomstalks are quite compact and the red flowers are a pleasant addition to the clumps. An easy species to grow.

S. atlanticum

S. *atlanticum* is the only species found in Africa, growing in the Atlas Mountains of Morocco. Klein and Kandereit (2015) concluded that this species was the result of a unique long-distance transport with subsequent speciation in Morocco. Despite coming from a climate quite different than Oregon, this has been a most handsome and reliable species. The rosettes are medium large and are a unique shade of pale green, almost luminous. For those who do not want the semps to flower, here is one for you. Mine has never flowered in five years of growth. There are several forms available. 'Ball's Form' has a bit more red flush to the leaves and its leaves are more incurved. I prefer the more green form, as it is such an attractive shade and contrasts well with red or purple cultivars.

S. ciliosum

I almost did not list this species here among the garden-worthy as it is a bit difficult to grow, especially if you live in a wet winter climate. S. *ciliosum* is one furry little devil, and all that fur in the wild serves the useful purpose of gathering bits of dew to supply the plant with much-needed moisture. This sponge-like aspect of the plant is what makes it a problem in wet climates. However, it is *so* cute it is well worth growing and even covering in a wet winter. The rosettes are small and the thin leaves are highly incurved, forming an almost spherical rosette heavily covered in hair. My favorite of these forms is the collection known as 'Ali Botusch,' which has a flush of a bright red that contrasts beautifully with the abundant cilia.

I crossed 'Ali Botusch' with 'Denise's Cobweb' a few years ago. The one seedling that persisted was an amazing mass of cilia, and although it was very cool, it had a death wish for survival in my wet winter climate. If I were to do it again, I would cross 'Ali Botusch' with something with far less cilia. Lesson learned.

Fig. 3-8. *S. ciliosum*

S. marmoreum

S. marmoreum is the very variable red-flowered diploid (chromosome count 34) species of the Balkans. What was formerly four species are now grouped under *S. marmoreum*. These include the globular form *ssp. balsii,* the finely velvety *ssp. erythraeum*, *ssp. marmoreum* with mainly ciliated rosettes, and the velvety form *reginae-amailae*. Any of these are nice plants for the garden, forming neat, compact clumps. One form from my youth, known then as 'Rubicundum' (= *S. marmoreum* 'Rubrifolium'), had small leaves of a very bright red edged neatly with green. Although Ed Skrocki mixed his seed, he believed it was the parent of his 'Rubikon' and 'Rubikon Improved,' the names being a nod to this *marmoreum* clone. It is likely other small red cultivars owe some of their heredity to this plant as well. Similarly, the 'Chocolate' (also known as 'Brunneifolium') form has lovely café-au-lait color, and this cultivar has imparted its soft brown colors to a number of cultivars. Both Nicholas Moore and Betty Bronow used forms of *S. marmoreum* in their breeding programs with great success.

S. marmoreum ssp. erythraeum is an interesting plant, and perhaps my favorite of the subspecies. This is a smallish rosette with a very fine, velvety surface to the leaf. The velvety texture of this species is a much finer pubescence than noted on *S. montanum*, and perhaps accounts for the soft, almost translucent color of the rosette. Rosettes are very compact and make a very neat clump. This is a plant that looks good all year long, with a slight red-purple flush to the rosettes, especially in the spring, in the clones from the Rila Mountains in Bulgaria. Representatives of this species from other areas appear to be more simple greens with darker tips (Stephenson and Stephenson 2016). This species merits more use as a parent of hybrids. This was one of Praeger's favorites and I agree with his decision.

NATURAL HYBRIDS

In the Alps, the five species described above cross with each other wherever their ranges overlap. Moreover, because many of the hybrids are fertile, they are able to cross among themselves and back to their parents (and any other semp blooming!). This makes for a very confusing lot, and is one of the reasons the taxonomy of the semps is such a mess. To create some order out of this chaos, grex (group names) were established for at least some of these hybrid combinations. The two most important in terms of our present day situation are the hybrids *S. barbulatum* (a cross of *S. montanum* with *S. arachnoideum*) and *S. x fauconnettii* (a cross of *S. tectorum* and *S. arachnoideum*), which are the two most common, but each of these has so many selections, it is probably better for them to be known as individual clones rather than the hybrid grex. It is difficult or impossible to tell whether these are primary hybrids or backcrosses to either parent without a detailed genetic analysis.

One especially nice hybrid described by Praeger is *S. x calcaratum*, which when growing semps as a youth was one of the most lovely cultivars available. It is probably at least partially derived from *S. tectorum* and *S. wulfenii*, but has a distinctive flush of lavender or purple and has relatively large rosettes and broad leaves. Some of the early named hybrids such as 'Rosy Purple Beauty' and 'Magnificum' appear similar to *S. x calcaratum*, and these cultivars have been involved in many of the smooth-leaved purples, lavenders, and other large-leaved glabrous cultivars. Because of *S. x calcaratum* we owe much to the development of our present day hybrids. Even Praeger, who disdained the hybrids, freely admitted how beautiful this plant is.

As with anything in life, tastes differ dramatically as to what species would be your favorites. If you are a purist rock gardener, only the species might be acceptable in your recreation of an Alpine landscape. If this describes you, then the many selections of the species in this chapter as well as *all* of the *S. heuffelii* cultivars and wild selections of the rollers should pass the purist's test. For the rest of us, give the species in this chapter a try before venturing into the more difficult and rare members.

REFERENCES

Dumont D, G Dumont (2013) "*Sempervivum calcareum* Jordan. Portrait of a misunderstood star." *Acta Succulenta* 1: 53–72

Klein JT, J W Kadereit (2015) "Phylogeny, biogeography, and evolution of edaphic association in the European oreophytes *Sempervivum* and *Jovibarba* (Crassulaceae)." *Int J Plant Sci* 176: 44–71

Mitchell PJ (1973) *The Sempervivum and Jovibarba Handbook*. The Sempervivum Society. Burgess Hill, UK

Mort EA, D E Soltis, P S Soltis, J Francisco-Ortega, A Santos-Guerra (2001) "Phylogenetic relationships and evolution of Crassulaceae inferred from *matK* sequence data." *Amer J Bot* 88: 76–91

Smith AC (1975) *The Genus Sempervivum and Jovibarba*. Published by author. Keston, Kent, UK

Smith MC (1981) "*Sempervivum (Crassulaceae)* in Spain and the Pyrennes." *Lagascalia* 10: 1-23

Stephenson R, J Stephenson (2016) "Succulents of the Balkan range, Bulgaria." *Sedum Society Newsletter* 119: 11–13

t'Hart H, Bleij B, B Zonneveld (2003) "Sempervivum." In: *Crassulaceae* (ed, U Eggli). Springer Verlag, Berlin: 332–349

Wills, H., S. Wills (2004) *An Introduction to Sempervivum and Jovibarba*. Species and Cultivars. Fernwood Nursery, UK

CHAPTER 4

RECOMMENDED CULTIVARS

With the thousands of hybrids available to gardeners and with new hybrids being produced each year, any list of choice *Sempervivum* cultivars is almost immediately out of date and virtually any aficionado will come up with a different list that they might think are the best. However, this list will give the potential gardener a number of fine plants that have proven themselves in my garden and in others.

This list is also biased a bit by what cultivars are available here in the US, although we have steadily been adding cultivars from Europe. Many of these new European cultivars are included among the recommended cultivars with the hopes that many will be on the market.

In the list, the cultivars are divided into types, so if the reader wants a particular type of plant for a particular use, it will be easier to find just that right plant. Betty Bronow used a similar classification in her *The Perennial Garden* catalogs, and it is a good way to group and compare the cultivars.

GLABROUS OR SATIN CULTIVARS

Many of the cultivars have either no obvious hairs or are truly without hairs. These cultivars are often better for areas where growth of semps is more of a problem in terms of rotting, as they generally have the very rot-resistant *S. tectorum* somewhere in the pedigree.

— PRIMARILY GREEN —

Although you might think of green cultivars as boring, these cultivars listed below are anything but. Moreover, these lighter shades are really useful at planting beside reds and purples, as it sets them off. Also included are several unusual shades of green. These colors really *pop*.

'Rita Jane' (MacPherson)

Sandy MacPherson selected many cultivars from seedlings that appeared among his plantings. 'Rita Jane' was selected for its very wide leaves of an unusual shade of olive, flushed with pink, and with deep purple tips. Bronze Rosette winner in England and a very hardy and easy-to-grow plant.

'Olivette' (Skrocki)

'Olivette' has such a unique shade of green, really resembling unripe olives in a rosette of medium to medium-large size. The leaves are rounded and slightly incurved, so the visual effect of the plant is also like an olive. This plant can be a little temperamental, so give it a bit better drainage and/or grit placed around the plant to protect it from splash-back.

Fig. 4-1. 'Olivette'

'Plastic' (Skrocki)

What a great name, and so apropos for this plant. Most semps have relatively thin leaves, but 'Plastic' has chubby and very sturdy leaves that remind one more of some *Aeonium* or *Echevaria* cultivars. The leaf is a pastel green with a bit of pink at the base. It is the shape that sets this plant apart. Plant this cultivar where you can observe it at close range so the unique form is more obvious.

'California' (Geiger)

If you like small ones with unique forms then this is for you. It is like 'Plastic,' in that the leaves are chubbier than normal, but in 'California,' the rosettes are much smaller and the leaves are quite short, making it very chubby. This is one of my favorites of Erwin's creations. Because of its small size, it is one that you need to grow in an area where you can observe it easily or grow it in pot culture.

'Uranus'

One of my pet peeves is a visitor who comes to my garden and points to the lovely rosettes of 'Uranus' and says, "Oh I have *that* one," and you know darn well they are referring to *S. tectorum*, not this really beautiful contrasted green with inky purple tips and medium-large rosettes. The green color of 'Uranus' is rather luminous and the rosette shape is very pleasing, too. This is no ordinary *tectorum*!

'Sharon's Pencil' (Vaughn)

This unusual name comes from my recurrent borrowing of a friend's pencil in high school. This cultivar is that sort of "pencil green" color and it has rather narrow leaves. This can get *huge* too; it has grown to nine inches in diameter for me. It blooms rather heavily in the UK, but it is not especially that way here in the US. This is one of the few green seedlings out of the open-pollinated 'Silverine' group and had a form unlike all the others too.

'Nico' (Haberer) and 'Fernwod' (Wills)

These two cultivars are bright green with bright red tips to the leaves. The leaves are incurved and are quite sharply pointed, so the red tips are really accentuated. The shades of green and tone of red are different, and both are very attractive plants.

'Jade' (Rollich)

There is a *heuffelii* selection also named this—but this is the semp. A very bright jade green color, although sometimes the outer leaves are a distinctive bright scarlet that further sets off the jade green center. This rosette is medium to large and a very healthy grower.

'Emerald Giant' (Wood) and 'Emerson's Giant'

To me, the "giant" part of these names is a bit of a misnomer, as I have lots of semps that are as big or bigger. Both of these are green with purple tips, and are so similar that I often wonder if they are not in fact the same plant. 'Emerson's Giant' grows a bit bigger for me, so it gets the nod as the better of the two if I had to decide.

'Wilhelm Tell' (Smits)

William Tell is one of the national heroes of Switzerland, and this semp from a Swiss hybridizer honors that hero. My plant came from our local Swiss transplant, Urs Baltenberger, with the comment, "This is one you need." Basically, this is a medium-sized rosette in bright green with sharp points that are accented by very strong, deep purple tips. A neat grower that has few problems. Similar plants include "Café" and many others, although this is one of the best of this color combination.

'Purdy's 70-40' (Purdy)

This was one of my favorites as a kid and it is still a nice semp. An unusual shade of green (not quite olive, but close) with relatively wide rosettes and tiny purple tips. As are all these numbered seedlings, these were distributed from Purdy's extensive collection after his death. As a hybridizer I would really like to know the pedigree of this plant. Produces seedlings with very wide leaves.

'Jolly Green Giant' (Nixon)

This was an unnamed plant that was being distributed by several nurseries in Massachusetts. Bill Nixon picked out this most appropriately named cultivar. It can grow to six inches in diameter and is a most unique green, as the leaves are strongly watermarked, almost with a powdered look. The form on this plant is lovely, with broad leaves that are tapered wider in the middle and with a pronounced thorny tip.

'Lilac Time' (Milton)

This plant is a little difficult to classify. It is basically a waxy green with a broad, soft, lilac-pink base to each leaf. The rosette is large and has an open "waterlily" form that shows off this pink base to the leaf especially well. This plant can be a bit prone to rotting, so plant in a place with good drainage and/or add pea gravel around the plant. This has been an especially interesting parent, and I have some lovely dark blends from 'Lilac Time' X 'Jungle Shadows.' 'Lilac Time' was given an Award of Garden Merit (AGM) by the Royal Horticultural Society. A very deserving winner.

Fig. 4-2. 'Lilac Time'

'Michael' (Vaughn)

This was my version of 'Lilac Time,' although 'Michael' pre-dates 'Lilac Time' and is maybe a bit bigger too. It has the same sort of "waterlily form" that I find most attractive, a pastel silvery green with pale pink leaf bases. In the winter, this cultivar turns a lovely shade of raspberry, so it is one of my favorites for winter color. This cultivar appeared as a volunteer seedling in my rock garden in Massachusetts and may be a seedling of 'Silvertone,' as it was found near that plant.

'Tristesse' (van der Steen)

An interesting shade of sort of slate green with brownish-purple leaf tips. The rosette is very solid and has a very compact habit, so the center of the rosette looks very brown, as only the leaf tips are obvious. The form of the rosette resembles some of the forms of S. *cantabricum*, although as far as I know the parentage of this plant is unknown. 'Tristesse' won both an Award of Merit from the Sempervivum Society and an AGM from the Royal Horticultural Society. Although this is not a flashy cultivar, it has become one of my favorites.

'Reinhard' (Haberer)

A very neat plant of medium green with strongly contrasted nearly black tips. The leaves are rather sharply pointed and upright, accentuating this effect. The colors in this cultivar are good all year round, and it is a good contrast to darker or yellowish rosettes. This cultivar is descended from *S. cantabricum*, but does not appear to be a pure form, rather a hybrid.

'Elene' (Payne)

This is one that Helen secretly tried to name for herself, using the foreign name for Helen (Elena), but also substituting an "e" for the terminal "a" to further disguise this bit of immortality. 'Elene' has long satin leaves of a dark olive green with a strong pink flush and purple leaf tip. The leaf edges are fringed with rather long cilia that give the leaf a more frosted look because of the wide open form of the rosette. This plant seems to have several imposters being sold as the real cultivar.

'Lion King' (Wills)

This is a hard cultivar to place. It is a large rosette with prominent purple brown tips and the remainder of the leaf is a blend of brown and green. The incurved leaves give the center a sort of prominent brown-purple eye that really contrasts with the remainder of the leaf. A very solid plant and a unique one. Its size and striking but subtle colors always attract attention. My favorite from this hybridizer and a plant that should be better known.

Fig. 4-3. 'Lion King'

'Serena' (Skrocki)

Ed lived in an old house in Hinckley, Ohio, and he was convinced it was haunted by a spirit he called "Serena." This semp is an homage to this spirit. Medium-sized leaves of a sort of khaki green have rust red tips and centers. This is one that produces fasciated rosettes rather often and they can be spectacular.

'Pax' (Haberer)

This one I was tempted to put in the red group, as there are times of the year when this can be reddish, but for most of the year it is green. 'Pax' is a very neat cultivar with smallish rosettes with multiple leaves that form a very rounded, button-like structure. It just screams *cute*. A very easy cultivar to grow. The pinkish flowers on short stems are in good proportion to the smallish plants.

'Carmen' (Payne)

This cultivar was one of Helen's favorites and rightly so. It is a big green rosette with wide leaves that have a brilliant red tip and leaf backs. This brilliant red tip contrasts beautifully with the light green color of the remainder of the rosette. A nice sturdy grower that will reward the gardener.

— SILVER, BLUE, TO GREY —

This is a diverse group, containing basically green plants with flushes of color and powdery wax that pushes them over to silver, grey, or blue. These are more subtle colors and are good for balancing out darker colors and reds.

'Grey Lady' (Vaughn)

'Grey Lady' was one of the many hundreds of seedlings I grew from 'Silverine' seed that was open-pollinated, and was the only one of the group with this grey color and purple tips. The rosettes are only medium-sized compared to the much larger rosettes of its pod parent. This is a good semp to use to contrast with bright purples or reds.

'Silverine' (MacPherson)

Sandy MacPherson named several plants with the color plus "ine" added to the name. 'Silverine' was the first cultivar that was really silver in color, due to its waxy overlay to the basic blue-green leaf color. Its form and relatively few increases are indicative of some *S. wulfenii* in the pedigree. Some of its seedlings show that sort of conical bud that typifies *S. wulfenii* as well. 'Silverine' is a large rosette, and coupled with its silver color makes excellent contrast to the darker colors. The seedlings from this plant were almost uniformly excellent. I named eight cultivars from 'Silverine,' either through hand crosses or open-pollinated seed. A sport or variation of this plant that was found among the 'Silverine' stock plants at Mountain Crest Gardens has been named 'Pinkerine' by our friends there in California, as it is a much pinker version.

'Soul' (Ford)

This is David's improved version of 'Silverine.' The rosettes are a bit smaller, but the plant is more robust, and the silver color holds for more of the season. This is one that deserves to be better known. A very nice plant. David also named a *heuffelii* cultivar 'Soul'; this was allowed because at the time of his naming the plant the two groups were different genera.

'Silver Song' (Vaughn)

Many years ago I raised several hundred seedlings of 'Silverine.' The seedlings were almost all very nice. The one I named 'Silver Song' was my pick of the more silvery-toned ones. When it was a small seedling, the leaf bases were flushed a lovely peach pink, and it sometimes shows this peach color even now. The remainder of the rosette is a very clear silver, and the form of the rosette more resembles *S. wulfenii* than its mom. I had not used 'Silver Song' as a parent until I retired and moved to Oregon, but the seedlings from it have been quite beautiful. At least one of these seedlings will be named in the near future.

Fig. 4-4. 'Silver Song'

'Blue Boy' (Vaughn)

The production of semps with bluish tints has proven to be difficult, and the term "blue" is mainly in our imagination, or as a flush of color rather than a real blue. 'Blue Boy' is a seedling of Helen Payne's 'Thayne,' which showed some blue tints, but 'Blue Boy' has much more of that tint, especially in the summer. This is a very prolific cultivar and an easy grower.

'Pacific Blue Ice' (Gossett)

This is Gary's entry into the area of "blue" semps and is a really nice addition to the group. The medium-sized rosettes are a good frosty blue-green with a touch of lavender that seems to set the color off and with small deeper tips. Easy grower and a nice plant.

Fig. 4-5. 'Pacific Blue Ice'

'Frost and Flame' (Vaughn)

Of the seedlings from the open-pollination of 'Silverine,' the bluest selection was the cultivar I named 'Minaret.' Open-pollinated seed from 'Minaret' gave a number of much more blue seedlings. 'Frost and Flame' was the bluest, as well as the largest of the seedlings in this group. A very vigorous plant and easy grower. The seedlings from this plant are the bluest and largest I have yet produced, but this is a slow process increasing the blue color.

'Aqua' (Elliot)

Emma Elliot runs Wild Ginger Farm Nursery in Oregon, which features a number of rare and unusual plants. She has also selected out a number of very interesting semp seedlings. 'Aqua' is quite unique. A broad-leaved flat rosette with a lot of blue tints from a sort of light purple comingling with the silvery base color. Good grower and very hardy.

'Sandi Lu' (Vaughn)

This seedling was spotted by Sandi Bagley in my seedling bed during one of the Hybridizers' Clinics as having exceptionally broad leaves and an unusual color of gray with purple tips. As the seedling matured it has kept a very distinctive look and makes a very pretty neat mound. Sandi was happy that I named this selection for her and she suggested the name 'Sandi Lu.' It makes me smile every time I see it, thinking of my friend in Colorado.

◄ **Fig. 4-6.** 'Sandi Lu'

▶ **Fig. 4-7.** 'Blue Whale'

▼ **Fig. 4-8.** 'Blue Balou'

'Blue Whale' (Vaughn)

No surprise how this name came about. It is big and very blue-hued with just a tiny tip of purple. This cultivar tends to get blue earlier than many of the others. The rosettes have a lovely shape and the plant is vigorous and of easy culture.

'Blue Balou' (Graf)

This is a new one from Europe that I think is wonderful. The rosettes are medium-sized and a very cool shade of blue-green, very perfectly formed, with wide leaves with very symmetrical rosettes. Can't wait to use this one as a parent.

— YELLOW-GREEN —

Several semps have tints of gold color to them of varying amounts. Plant these next to dark greens or purples to accentuate the color differences in these ones that tend toward yellow.

'Pink Lemonade' (Bishop)

'Pink Lemonade' was from a group of open-pollinated seedlings of 'Magnificum,' itself one of the nicer semps of the '60s, and it was the only one that had tints of yellow or mustard. The leaves are strongly flushed pink at the base, which was the inspiration for the name. This was the first non-*Jovibarba* that had yellow in the rosettes too and was a breakthrough at the time. The yellow color is fleeting and is soil/temperature/sun affected.

'Bernstein' (Botanical Garden of Tubingen)

Again, this is not yellow, but a sort of chartreuse to olive with deeper tips to the leaves. This is a good, vigorous plant that makes a good clump in a hurry. It can get quite large. The best yellow color occurs in the spring and it becomes more of a light green by summer.

'Mitchell's Gold'
(believed to be the same as 'Michael's Golden')

This is a slower grower, but it has a lot of lighter yellow-green colors, especially in the spring. The compact plants have deeper tips to the leaves that set off the color. This plant has struggled in my yard, tries to bloom out, and in general is not happy. The coloration is worth the extra effort and several local growers have no problems. It does not like me, though, even as much I like it.

'Sassy Frass' (Skrocki)

The name shows Ed Skrocki's sense of whimsy in naming his plants, a play on the name of the sassafras tree. This cultivar has sort of a tawny rosette. The rosettes are small to medium, but this is a fast increaser and makes a nice clump quickly. There are some imposters of this plant in circulation that do not have the tawny color.

'Butterbur' (Bronow)

Fig. 4-9. 'Butterbur'

This is quite a unique plant, in that the rosettes often produce fasciate rosettes that add to the diversity of the clump. Unlike most fasciated forms, the ones on 'Butterbur' do not expand a great deal, leading to a clump with a variety of shapes. The rosette is large and flat, but the individual leaves are rather short, but numerous and wide, leading to an interesting look even if the rosettes are not fasciated. The color is sort of tawny, an olive green with mustard highlights and pink bases, with the rosette becoming distinctly purple when it begins to bolt with a bloomstalk. 'Butterbur' is a seedling from Ed Skrocki's 'Collage' open pollinated and is an improvement upon its parent. This is one to plant where it can be easily seen so that the diversity of rosette forms and colors are more obvious. Betty's reasons for choosing this name for this cultivar show her imagination and personality:

> Perhaps 'Butterbur' is the most appropriately named hybrid of my Tolkein family. Barliman Butterbur, the inn keeper at The Prancing Pony at Bree, was a short fat man with a bald head and red face. Anyone can apply those characteristics to S. 'Butterbur,' but more subtle are the two changes both Butterburs are noted for. Barliman is a jovial and rather lovable while serving his famous beer, but changes to a stupid, forgetful (but still lovable) landlord in a crisis. Namesake, S. 'Butterbur' also makes two changes without taking on the drab dormant look of most semps. (Bronow 1986)

'Goldmarie' (Geiger)

This can get *very* large and is very exciting all season with its very pointed leaves. In spring, the rosettes are heavily flushed rose, giving an almost orange effect. In the summer, the red tones disappear, leaving a bright gold rosette. This has been a very happy increaser and much better grower than most of the other yellowish semps. A real winner.

◄ **Fig.4-10**. 'Goldmarie'

▼ **Fig. 4-11.** Chick Charms® 'Gold Nugget'

Chick Charms® 'Gold Nugget' (Hansen)

Wow! This is a sport of my 'Ruby Heart' in a fairly bright gold with prominent red tips. Unlike many plants with this much yellow, 'Gold Nugget' is a strong grower, seemingly with all the vigor, increase, and size of 'Ruby Heart.' One of the surprising things about this semp is that the red coloration is at the leaf tip instead of the leaf base. As a proud grandfather I cannot recommend this plant enough! The star of the Chick Charms® line.

— GREEN AND RED BICOLORS —

This is one of the gaudier groups of semps and one of my favorites. The colors can be bright or more subdued, but these are great conversation pieces in the bed. Most of these have red bases, but a few of these are flushed red at the top of the leaves, not the bottom.

'Persephone' (Smits)

This my favorite of Smit's hybrids, and certainly in my top ten for all semps. A huge rosette with exceptionally broad leaves in medium green with a bright red-purple base. Even when the red color fades, it is still an impressive cultivar because of the width of its leaves and size of the rosettes. The bloomstalk on this cultivar is *huge* too. I can't wait to use this cultivar in crossing. My friend Lynn Smith has gotten the jump on me using this plant as a parent.

Fig. 4-12. 'Persephone'

'Killer' (Schara)

When I moved to Oregon, I discovered a wonderful nursery run by a wonderful and talented Swiss nurseryman, Urs Baltenberger, who brought some of the best semps from Europe with him. 'Killer' was one of this group I bought at first sight. This is a great plant, but a very changeable one. It can appear as a red-green bicolor, all red, and all green depending on the season, and some of these guises are very bright. The rosettes are medium-sized and the leaves are sharply pointed, giving the rosette a spiky appearance. This is an amazing parent, giving a wide variety of sizes and shapes to its seedlings, as well as some unique, very intense colors.

'Marshall' (Vaughn) and 'Ruby Heart' (Vaughn)

These two are sister seedlings from the open pollination of 'Silverine.' Both are attempts to make a large silver-colored rosette with red bases. Neither are my final ideal plant toward this goal. 'Marshall' has more silver but less red and 'Ruby Heart' has more red but less silver. Both are nice plants and vigorous growers. There are seedlings from both of these cultivars being evaluated that may be steps closer to my goal. Although the seed collected from 'Silverine' was open pollinated, it is likely that 'Engle's Rubrum' was the pollen parent, as it was blooming next to the 'Silverine' plant.

'Heart of Darkness' (Vaughn)

This semp could fall in the purple group too, but it really is a bicolor of green with a very large base of deep red-purple that makes for a highly contrasted and showy combination. 'Heart of Darkness' combines 'Killer' and 'Jungle Shadows,' and has some of the best

Fig. 4-13. 'Heart of Darkness'

aspects of both of its parents: the pattern from 'Killer' and the more intense and larger size from 'Jungle Shadows.' The seedlings from this plant have been amazing, especially in crosses to 'Borscht.'

'Harlequin Rouge' (Elliot)

Hybridizer Emma Elliot gardens in Beavercreek, Oregon, and this semp is one of her best. 'Harlequin Rouge' is a large plant that is green with very bright red leaf bases. The form is more upright, and it has many leaves that add to its distinction. Like all of Emma's hybrids, an easy grower and very hardy, trouble-free plant.

Fig. 4-14.
'Harlequin Rouge'

'Glowing Embers' (Skrocki) and 'Flasher' (Vaughn)

These are very similar and may be related, as I used one of Ed's seedlings (#51) as a parent of 'Flasher.' Both of these are very bright, basically a green rosette with all the outer leaves heavily flushed a brilliant scarlet to tangerine-pink. 'Glowing Embers' is larger, but both are at least medium-sized. These are both show stoppers in the bed and add lots of color. Plant these next to pastel varieties to enhance the contrast.

'Mulberry Wine' (Vaughn)

Ed Skrocki and I shared seedlings that might be useful in breeding, and one he shared with me was #51. It had very bright color, but was not a very satisfactory plant, as the form was irregular and it could rot. I crossed some of the flowers with my 'Minaret,' which has really perfect form and no tendency to rot. I did not separate out the crossed flowers with the open pollinated ones, so there are some that are from 'Minaret,' but others are not. 'Mulberry Wine' looks to be a much better formed and more intense version of Ed's #51. It has very strongly marked red-purple leaf bases and sort of a chartreuse yellow leaf tip, making for very good contrast. The color lasts well and it is an overall good garden plant.

'Roasted Chestnut' (Vaughn)

In the spring, this semp has the most brilliant chestnut brown infused red at the tips of all the leaves. A very good increaser and very hardy plant. Later in the season it converts to a green rosette with red tips. When I started growing and breeding semps again in Oregon Erwin Geiger kindly sent me some mixed seed, and there were several nice ones from this seed, but only 'Roasted Chestnut' was named.

➤ **Fig. 4-15.** 'Roasted Chestnut'

◄ **Fig. 4-16.** 'Gingerbread Boy'

'Gingerbread Boy' (Mylin)

This is sort of like a much bigger version of 'Glowing Embers' and 'Flasher,' a green with strong red tips, especially on the back of the leaves. The form of the rosette is more upright, which really shows off the showy red-tipped leaf backs.

'Fire Glint' (Moore)

This English hybrid has the same sort of color distribution as 'Roasted Chestnut,' but the colors are different, more red than brown in 'Fire Glint.' This is a very showy plant and one that should be in more gardens. It can get big when it is very happy, making it even showier.

— "PINKS" —

Pink is mostly mythical in *Sempervivums*. The following selections are plants that have some pink tints to them. Some are very pale reds, lavenders, or purples that give the effect of pink. Many hybridizers are working toward these shades, and some of the newer offerings are a bit closer to the color than others. In my program, I have been trying to extend the pinkish leaf base colors farther up the leaf. Several of these are under observation now (Fig. 4-11).

Fig. 4-17. A pink seedling of the author's scheduled for introduction.

78

'Pacific Taffy Pink' (Gossett)

Taffy pink is a good descriptor for this plant, as it sort of has a pale tan color with a flush of pink to it. The medium-sized rosettes have good increase.

'Slabber's Seedling' (Slabber)

No one seems to know exactly who Slabber is, but this is an interesting cultivar nonetheless. The rosettes are medium large and an odd mix of grey and pink, with the pink stronger toward the leaf edges. As the leaves become very mature they turn a bright pink, just before they go senescent. The effect is bits of bright pink scattered across the clump. This cultivar produces rather thick stolons on its increase that support the offset for a longer period than most.

'Thunder' (Skrocki)

I am not sure why Ed named this cultivar 'Thunder,' as you would expect something *bold* with that name; 'Thunder' is not. This is a very soft, light olive rosette with the leaves flushed pink about two-thirds of the length of the leaf.

'Flamingo' (Skrocki)

This was one of the first I could say, "Yes, that is pink." The leaves on this one are long and very pointed. The olive green leaves flush a quite true pink in spring. Can get large.

'Pacific Jordan' (Gossett)

This cultivar has not gotten much press, but I find it a really nice plant. In spring it is sort of a strawberry pink, but with a waxy sheen that makes it appear almost creamy. The color transforms to sort of a blue silver with a pink infusion to the center of the rosette in the summer. Very wide leaves and nice shape.

'Gwen's Rose' (Vaughn)

The cross of ('Killer' X self) gave all sorts of lovely colors and plant types. This seedling was one of the bigger ones in the cross. It is extremely variable in color, going from a sort of strawberry pink to a frosted rose red during the season. I had sent this plant to Toby Landers under number and he liked it so well he asked it be named for his new daughter Gwen.

◄ **Fig. 4-18.** 'Gwen's Rose'

— VARIEGATED FORMS —

Up until quite recently there were very few variegated forms available, although variegated *Aeoniums* have been known for years. Both Ed Skrocki and Bill Nixon found variegated sports in their plantings, but none of these were vigorous or stable. These new ones are much more stable and vigorous, adding an exciting dimension to the semp cultivars available.

'Saxon' (Lazlo Szakszon)

From our friend in Hungary comes this light green with a distinctive edge to each leaf. This displays the leaf edging that we typically see in variegated leaf chimeras in other genera in which one of the histogenic layers of the meristem is genetically albino. This stable arrangement of tissue makes for a healthy plant with very even cream margins. Can't wait for this plant to be available worldwide. It looks to be a mutation of some sort of *tectorum* based upon the morphology of the plant, but may have other species involved as well.

'Brillante' (Noyes and Mylin)

'Brillante' was first discovered by Janis Noyes and her mother Joyce Hoekstra in a plant of 'Rocknoll Rosette' and then selected over the years by Don Mylin to make a stable clone. The stripe of red down the center of the leaf sets off the very clean and relatively broad white edge. The leaves appear to be thinner than 'Rocknoll Rosette,' but other characteristics are similar. Although it is not a fast grower, it increases better than many variegated plants and is a showy and unique specimen for your collection.

➤ **Fig. 4-19.** 'Saxon'

Fig. 4-20. 'Brillante'

'Red Lion Variegated'

This plant is not a chlorophyll mutation, but rather the green leaves have irregular splashes of red. No two rosettes are alike, and offsets will vary on a single plant from all red to all green. A fun conversation piece.

— REDS AND PURPLES —

In this section I have lumped the reds and purples into one class, as many of the reds have a bit of purple tint and all of the purples have some red in their coloring as well. However, within these groups there are some that are decidedly red and some decidedly purple. Some of the most recent cultivars approach black in coloration. Many older cultivars in this group fade to green in the summer, but more recent cultivars tend to hold their color through much of the year or change to other attractive shades.

'Lavender and Old Lace' (Payne)

This plant was a major breakthrough when it first appeared. It has a distinctive rosy-lavender color that was a flush on the top two-thirds of each leaf with a green base. The leaves have a strong cilia, giving them a frosted appearance. Helen once confessed to me that this plant actually came in a shipment of plants from Sandy MacPherson, as he was not religious in moving bloomstalks from the plantings so that seedlings would often occur with the other plant. Being frugal, Helen separated these seedlings from the other plants and eventually named any that appeared to be interesting. 'Lavender and Old Lace' received a Gold Rosette from the Sempervivum Society. Two of its seedlings—'Risqué' and 'Bedazzled'—are more intense versions with larger rosettes than their mom.

'Jewel Case' (Skrocki)

A very nice medium to large sized rosette in an odd blend of colors which is more intense toward the center of the rosette. Betty Bronow described it as, "hues of jade, onyx, and amber overlaid with burnt sienna." This is one that can have a problem in wet winters, but it is worth a little bit more effort. Keep it dry and mulch with gravel.

'Aldo Moro' (van der Steen)

This plant is difficult to place, as it has quite an array of colors: green, orange, red, and purple can at certain times of the year predominate. Regardless of the time of the year, the tips are much darker, at times approaching black. The medium-sized

Fig. 4-21. 'Lavender and Old Lace'

rosettes are healthy and produce good increase. This is a cross of two *S. tectorum* clones 'Atropurpureum' X 'Nigrum.'

'Fuego' (Haberer)

'Fuego,' as the name implies, is *hot*! A very bright red rosette with smaller tips of green. Can grow very large and is a good grower, although it does not produce a lot of offsets. This is one of my favorite reds, although it is a less exciting parent than I had hoped.

'Othello' (Sponnier)

This is an older cultivar, but it is still very well worth growing. A very bright red, with the rosettes getting as big as six inches in diameter. The bloomstalks on this plant are enormous, and the flower is bigger than most with a brighter red color than most large *Sempervivum*. This is sometimes sold as 'Red Lion' in the US, but they are different plants.

'Jungle Shadows' (Vaughn)

'Jungle Shadows' was my first really important hybrid, as it has a rather unique color of a blend of greys and purples, large size (six inches plus), and most importantly, color that lasted for most of the year. When this seedling first occurred in my garden in 1968, this combination of characteristics was really unique. 'Jungle Shadows' was named after a border bearded iris that has a similar somber mélange of dark colors. Although I have always listed the pedigree as unknown, it was found near my clump of 'Silvertone' and near where I had pollinated the stalk the season previous with 'Atroviolaceum Heimlich'; it is most likely this cross. The seedlings from self-pollinating 'Jungle Shadows' gave some seedlings similar to these two putative parents. When I sent this plant to Helen Payne to introduce, Helen called and said, "Oh Kevin, we can sell *lots* of that one." She was very right. It won the Silver Rosette from the Sempervivum Society in 1976. As nice a plant as it is, it is even more valuable as a parent. It transmits all of its good qualities and has some very interesting genetic goodies. It is the parent of 'Jungle Fires,' 'Jungle Pimpernel,' 'Polly Bishop,' 'Helen Payne,' and 'Borscht,' among others.

'Jungle Fires' (Vaughn)

'Jungle Fires' was my first seedling from 'Jungle Shadows' and is from open pollination, although the likely pollen parent was 'Skrocki 51,' a seedling of Ed Skrocki's with a bright red-purple color. I put this pollen on the plant, but did not cover the flowers after crossing. This

➤ **Fig. 4-22.** 'Jungle Shadows'

◀ **Fig. 4-23.** 'Jungle Fires'

hybrid has the color of the putative pollen parent, but in form and size is more like 'Jungle Shadows.' It has better color retention than most and is a very easy grower. 'Jungle Fires' was used as a parent by Betty Bronow to create some of her Lord of the Rings series semps.

'Pacific Shadows' (Gossett)

Gary found 'Jungle Shadows' to be a useful parent, too, and this is his seedling from it. 'Pacific Shadows' is a bit darker, more purple than grey, than its mom, but otherwise is similar in shape and size. Like mom, this is a very easy grower and makes a very nice clump in the garden.

'Pacific Blazing Star' (Gossett)

A very neat plant. Long, narrow pointed leaves are a bright red in spring. By summer, the color has shifted a bit to more of a green with red highlights. Very showy and different.

'Missouri Rose' (Drown-Warner)

This is my favorite of Pat's hybrids. It is a medium-large plant with an unusual shade of rose, with almost a silvered look, and also has good watermarks. In the Pacific Northwest, this cultivar colors up late in the season and has lovely color from the end of July until winter, when others have faded. In Massachusetts it colored in the spring like other cultivars, but did retain its color fairly long. Its seedling 'Prairie Sunset' is similar, but has more yellow and brown tones added.

'Grunrand' (von Stein-Zeppelin)

This is a very slow-growing cultivar, but it is also *spectacular*! It can get huge, and has very wide leaves of a bright rose red neatly edged in green. I had the privilege of meeting Helen during one of her trips to America as she was visiting with the iris giant Bee Warburton. She was an amazingly refined and lovely person, and was responsible for importing many of the best of the American semps to Europe.

'Junimond' (Schara)

Here is another spectacular one that is also a slower grower. My plant came from my Swiss friend Urs Baltenberger, and he remarked on its beauty, but "it's not a commercial item." Too bad, as it is gorgeous. A very large rosette with a very intense red center and the outlying leaves are red. I did get seed on this plant one year, but decided not to grow them, as I did not want to be cursed with beautiful plants that would not increase. 'Junimond' is a seedling of 'T'Boz.'

'Plumb Rose' (Bishop) and 'Dark Cloud' (Bishop)

Polly Bishop put the bloomstalks of all of the darkest purple rosettes in a crisscrossed pattern so that the bees would cross all of these cultivars in every combination. The logic was that we really did not understand the genetics of dark color, and random matings between the darkest clones should allow for combinations of genes that make very dark rosettes. She then grew all the seed from these bee crosses and obtained roughly 300 seedlings. Many of these seedlings were advances in color and shape, but only these two cultivars were named that she considered the most distinctive. (How I wish we had some of the others for breeding now!) Both are large to very large rosettes. 'Dark Cloud' is a very dark grey heavily flushed with silver and banded in dark purple. The rosette has wide leaves that lie very flat. A fasciated rosette of this plant was over a foot in length! 'Plumb Rose' was Polly's favorite. It is a very dark purple, but has a sort of gauze-like overlay. The leaves of 'Plumb Rose' are quite pointed and the rosette has many leaves. 'Plumb Rose' is sometimes sold under the incorrect name 'Plum Rose.' Both of these cultivars are very easy growers and are favorites of growers all over the world.

Fig. 4-24. 'Dark Cloud'

'New Rhumba' (Mylin)

What a cool little plant! The leaves are very narrow and bright red edged with what looks like silver. I am not sure if it is variegated or just that the red color ends very neatly, making it appear variegated. The rosettes are small and it is not a fast grower, but is so cool you must have it. This occurred as a sport at SMG Succulents.

Fig. 4-25. 'New Rhumba'

'Director Jacobs' (van der Steen)

A medium-sized rosette with incurved leaves of a glowing deep red. The cilia along the leaf edge are prominent and white, making for a good contrast, and this effect is enhanced by the relatively incurved leaves. One that holds its color well all year.

'Rubikon' and 'Rubikon Improved' (Skrocki)

When I first started growing semps this was a cultivar then called 'Rubicundum,' a small red rosette with green edges to the leaves. We now know that 'Rubicundum' is really a form of *S. marmoreum*. These two semps of Ed Skrocki's were improvements over 'Rubicundum'; 'Rubikon Improved' was selected as a better plant than the original. Both forms suffer from winter wet conditions, but in the Midwest and East these are both good plants for the garden, providing good bright red color in a smaller rosette.

'Rosebud' (Vaughn)

Normally I do not breed smaller plants, and this was one of several smaller seedlings that arose from self-pollination of the much larger 'Killer.' Unlike 'Killer,' or its sister seedling 'Red Hot Chili,' this has a very rounded leaf form and a nearly solid rose-red rosette. In keeping with the smaller stature of this plant, the bloomstalk is much shorter and nicely proportioned to the height of the plant. This one is cute, but unfortunately a slow grower.

'Purple Dazzler' (Thomas)

A very large rosette of a good, bright, deep purple with green tips to the leaves. It is almost a bicolor of green and purple, but at least part of the year it is almost all purple as it grows here in Oregon. When it is growing happily, it is one of my favorite of all hybrids. Although it is a good grower, it is sensitive to winter wet, so you might want to cover this one for best winter growth.

'Red Hot Chili' (Vaughn)

This is a cool little semp. A very dark red on small starry-shaped rosettes with a very waxy sheen that makes them look polished. This is from 'Killer' X self and has the good habits of its parent, but a more consistent color and a full red, rather than a red/green bicolor. A good, vigorous grower that makes a neat clump. The bloomstalks on this plant are shorter than most cultivars.

Fig. 4-26. 'Red Hot Chili'

➤ **Fig. 4-27.** 'Fashion Diva'

'Fashion Diva' (Vaughn)

This is a sibling to 'Red Hot Chili,' but is quite a different plant. First, it is a much darker and less shiny red, and the plant is much bigger and the rosette much more upright. Can have very pretty watermarks that are like ripples on a pool of red liquid. A very vigorous grower and an exceedingly easy plant to grow.

'Pacific Devil's Food' (Gossett)

What a great name for this plant, as the leaves really do look like rich red-brown devil's food cake! Best yet, the color lasts well all season, the plant is a very vigorous grower, and it suffers from no rotting problems. One of my top ten favorites, and one I often give to beginners, as it is such a foolproof plant. Plant this next to very pale cultivars to accentuate its dark color.

'Hot Cocoa' (Elliot)

This is another cultivar whose name says it all. A very good sort of pastel chocolate brown with medium-sized rosettes. Although the color is most intense in the spring, the color lasts very well. Bloomstalks on this one are not tall, so that can be left without spoiling the looks of the clump. This may be Emma's best cultivar. I am excited about using this cultivar as a parent.

'Dyke' (Ford)

David Ford introduced many fine hybrids, but I think this may be my favorite of his. A very brilliant shade of red-purple on a rosette with very wide leaves that lie relatively flat. The leaves have a glossy sheen that set off the color. The rosettes turn green in the winter, but are red for much of the year.

'Tarita' (Smits)

A very distinctive cultivar. The inner leaves have an interesting blend of reds and purples of a deep and intense shade contrasted by the grey-green outer leaves. A very neat clump, although it can be affected by winter wet more than other cultivars. Still worth the effort.

'Positively Glowing' (Vaughn)

The inspiration for this name came from a BBC reporter's description of the Duchess Kate, who was "positively glowing" in her pregnancy. This is a medium-sized rosette of the most unusual shade of glowing cranberry red, with shading from light at the leaf base to much darker at the tip of the rosette. Watermarks add to its appeal. During summer, the rosette becomes olive with orange-red markings. This is one of the many interesting seedlings from 'Killer' X self.

Fig. 4-28. 'Positively Glowing'

'Crispyn' (van der Steen)

There are two plants going under this name. Mine came from Fernwood Nursery in the UK and it is a beauty. A reddish purple over grey rosette with sharply pointed leaves and a medium rosette. Very neat clump.

'Round Midnight' (Mylin)

A very apt name. The round rosettes have chubby leaves that make for a compact plant, but it can also obtain a good size. The color is a very dark red with a bit of shine to the leaf. A very pretty plant, and maybe my favorite of the Mylin cultivars. It retains its color well into summer months, unlike most red cultivars.

'Pepito' (Dillmann)

This is one of the outstanding new imports from Germany. A brilliant shade of red purple that is quite different than the usual bright red of most. The rosette can get quite large and the outer leaves often have gold tones, especially in summer. I am excited about using this cultivar as a parent.

'Patent Leather Shoes' (Vaughn)

This cultivar approaches black and has that shiny sheen that made me think of ubiquitous black patent leather shoes worn by every school girl in the '60s. The leaves have a very tiny green tip that set off the remainder of the leaf color. 'Patent Leather Shoes' is a medium-sized cultivar with rather compact rosettes. Very different than its sister seedlings from the 'Killer' X 'Jungle Shadows' cross.

'Big Six-O' (Vaughn)

The biggest and reddest of all the seedlings from 'Killer,' and it retains its red color for almost all of the year. Wonderful plant habits, and the color lasts well throughout the season. When I hit sixty years of age and had fifty years of seedlings, I decided to christen this plant with the memories of hitting both of these benchmarks.

➤ **Fig. 4-29.** 'Patent Leather Shoes'

◀ **Fig. 4-30.** 'Big Six-O'

'Tesoro' (Schara)

This is one of the nicest of the new German cultivars. A medium-sized rosette with a brilliant mulberry center and green tips to each leaf. The open form of the rosette shows off the colors beautifully. A good, easy grower. This should be very popular when more generally available in the US. A seedling of 'Kiara.'

VELVET CULTIVARS

Leaves in the velvet cultivars are covered with a dense layer of very fine hairs, causing the leaf to resemble velvet. Because of this velvety texture, the colors of the rosettes appear to be much more somber or darker than if the leaf was glabrous. The plants with velvety texture are a bit more sensitive to extra moisture, so if you live in high winter wet areas, these are ones you might wish to cover during the wet winter season.

'Aymon Correvon' (Correvon)

This plant was originally named 'Correvon's Hybrid,' but was later renamed for Correvon's grandson, as there was also an *S. heuffelii* clone that bore this same name. Regardless of the name, this is a very nice plant, a medium large, velvety grey, heavily flushed with pink at the base and with prominent purple tips. It is believed to be a cross of *S. montanum* and *S. wulfenii*, and its odd-colored flowers (sort of yellow flushed with pink) are also suggestive of this. This is often confused with the two following entries.

Fig. 4-31. 'Aymon Correvon'

'Purdy's 90-1' (Purdy) and 'Engle's 13-2' (Engle)

Both of these are a bit smaller than 'Aymon Correvon' as they grow for me in Oregon, and the rosettes are more compact in form with shorter leaves. When plants were evaluated in the Dalton Project, none of the plants were allowed to bloom for fear that the seed would contaminate the clones, but these two cultivars have much more purple in the blossom than 'Aymon Correvon.' For many years, all of these clones were lumped under 'Aymon Correvon' or 'Correvon's Hybrid.' Helen Payne kept these clones separated, as she saw other differences that she felt were significant. Correvon visited Purdy in the 1930s, and had most of his collection sent to him, so it is likely 'Purdy's 90-1' is a seedling of 'Aymon Correvon.' Neither 'Purdy's 90-1' nor 'Engle's 13-2' has ever produced viable offspring for me, although I have gotten normal-appearing seed from 'Aymon Correvon.'

'Downland Queen' (Mitchell)

Peter Mitchell was more fond of the species than the hybrids, but his wife and he did create a few interesting plants from hand crosses, although this one may have been a selection that was named by them, rather than their own work. 'Downland Queen' has a pale greyish-green rosette, with the velvet overlay giving a very soft and appealing effect. This one seems to have good weather resistance for a velvet cultivar.

'Belladonna' (MacPherson)

This was one of my favorite cultivars when I was a kid. Although this is grey, it is a darker grey than 'Aymon Correvon' or 'Purdy's 90-1,' and it is flushed with pink, especially toward the tip. This can get quite large.

'Yvette' (Smits)

'Yvette' is green, with very strong purple tips, and is medium-sized. This makes a very tidy clump with few health issues. The flowers are much larger than most and are a pale yellow, reflecting its *S. grandiflorum* pedigree. It may be pure *S. grandiflorum*.

'Proud Zelda' and 'Unicorn' (Skrocki)

'Proud Zelda' is an interesting cultivar, as it has so many guises of color. In the spring, it has pretty velvety leaves of an odd grey-green shade with purple tips to the leaf. In the summer months, the grey seems to fade and yellow overtones are more prominent. These yellowish rosettes contrast nicely with the rose flowers. 'Unicorn' is similar, except it does not go nearly as grey, so the spring color has more mustard overtones that carry over into the summer color. Both plants are very vigorous and easy growers, especially for velvet cultivars.

— REDS AND PURPLES —

'Cleveland Morgan' (Morgan)

F. Cleveland Morgan was a patron of the arts in Montreal, and was also known for his extensive rock garden. His Siberian iris hybrids 'Caesar's Brother' and 'Tropic Night' were major developments, and the top award for Siberian irises is named for him. When I first started breeding semps, this was the premier semp in the red velvet class, and it is still a wonderful plant. Sort of an orange-red with very velvety leaves. It has proven to be a tremendous parent. Unlike many velvet-leaved cultivars, 'Cleveland Morgan' appears to be fairly resistant to rotting. Its flowers are a pleasing pink color.

'Lipstick' (Vaughn)

'Lipstick' is from open pollinated seed of the glabrous 'Silverine,' but that plant grew right next to a clump of 'Cleveland Morgan'; 'Cleveland Morgan' is undoubtedly the pollen parent, as 'Lipstick' looks like a much larger, wider, and more deep red version of 'Cleveland Morgan.' It is a brick red, slightly deeper at the tip and with a nice velvety texture. I have seen rosettes as large as nine inches in diameter. In partial shade, the rosette becomes more two-toned, with red inner leaves and green outer leaves. The flowers on this plant are also rather nice, a clean pink. This was a Bronze Rosette in 1976. This was my favorite of my early hybrids and still finds favor in my eyes.

Fig. 4-32. 'Lipstick'

'Ohio Burgundy' (Skrocki)

This is Ed's velvety red one. Although he did not know the pedigree of this plant, he believed it to be a seedling of 'Cleveland Morgan' and an improvement on that plant. It appears to be a larger version of 'Cleveland Morgan' with a bit darker color, more toward brick red. This is one of the most vigorous of the velvets and a nice garden plant. A Bronze Rosette in 1976.

'Packardian' (Skrocki)

One of Ed Skrocki's other passions besides his semps were his Packard automobiles. Like the large, sturdy Packards, this is a very large and sturdy semp in an unusual maroon and brown color. The shape is unusual too, as the leaves are very elongated. Although the parentage of this plant is unknown, it has a strong resemblance to 'Sanfordii,' a hybrid from Sanford's Nursery in New York, and it is likely at least one of the parents of 'Packardian.'

'Greenwich Time' (Vaughn)

'Greenwich Time' was from one of my first crosses ('Cleveland Morgan' X *S. calcareum*), and this hybrid has the characteristics of both parents. In the spring, the rosette is a nice velvety red-purple, but by midsummer looks like a velvety version of the pollen parent: green with strong purple tips. Blooms on this plant are very odd, sort of greenish-white with a small pink stripe. To date, I have not had viable seed from this plant, either from my own crosses or by open pollinations. It may be a triploid, a hybrid from a tetraploid velvet type X the diploid *S. calcareum*.

'Tamerlane' (Drown-Warner)

Pat made this cross in that very first season we started crossing plants. This was a cross of 'Sanford Hybrid' X *S. montanum* var. *stiriacum*, although the seed planted from this group also probably contained a few open pollinated seeds as well. 'Tamerlane' does have the sort of rosette one would expect from this cross: a red-brown with velvety and very narrow leaves, but numerous and incurved. It transforms over the season to a dark green with purple tips. The incurved leaves give a distinct purple "eye" to the rosette. It has distinct, very clear pink flowers. This plant has also been distributed as 'Tamberlane,' as originally listed in the Oakhill Gardens catalog, but this is the correct spelling. Pat originally named this plant 'Green and Purple Velvet,' but Helen changed the name, as she felt it had the unusual spring color that was not reflected in its original name. A sister seedling, 'Neoga's Delight,' looks more like the pollen parent but is bigger in all respects.

'The Flintstones' (Smits)

What a cool semp! This is a medium-sized rosette with numerous, extremely narrow velvety leaves. In the spring, the leaves are a lovely shade of maroon red. Later in the year, the rosette becomes a mix of red and green, generally with more red in the center. A very distinct cultivar and one that should be in every collection.

COBWEBS

This group contains the cultivars that have full cobwebs, not just tufts of hairs at the tip, like the tufted group. Some of these are not full *S. arachnoideum* in pedigree, but at least have the appearance of a full cobweb. Almost all of these have lovely rose pink-colored flowers on short stalks. The contrast between the snowy cobwebs over the rosettes with the rose pink flowers above is a great garden effect. Do not cut these bloomstalks off and enjoy these flowers! Here I am listing the ones that are either full cobwebs or mostly so. The most webbed of the tufted group sort of merge into this group. Some of the other full cobweb varieties are described under *S. arachnoideum* in the species section of this book.

'Kramer's Spinrad' (van der Steen)

This may be my favorite of the full cobwebs, even though it might have some non-*arachnoideum* blood in there as well. This cobweb has very wide leaves and a fairly full cobweb on a rosette that is very compact, and flatter to the ground than most. This is also bigger than most cobwebs, and the flowers are larger than normal, too, although they are the same lovely rose pink shade of other cobweb cultivars. This has given some very interesting seedlings.

'Emberley Pink' (Vaughn)

This was a volunteer seedling that I sent to Helen as a possible introduction and she chose the name. It is sort of a rose-pink flushed rosette in spring with a fairly full cobweb. Rosettes are small, make a lot of increase, and these are very easy garden plants.

'Pygmalion' (Ford)

As one might expect from its name, this is a tiny selection of *S. arachnoideum*, but it increases so rapidly, it makes a clump rather quickly. Dense white cobweb with the outer leaves strongly flushed red, making for a nice contrast.

'Hurricane' (Skrocki)

This looks to be a full cobweb, and I wondered at first why Ed named this one 'Hurricane.' The cobweb does seem to be a bit more displaced/disheveled, as though a hurricane has gone through your garden and rearranged the cobwebbing. Very neat plant and makes a beautifully neat clump.

➤ **Fig. 4-33.** 'Pygmalion'

◄ **Fig. 4-34.** 'Hurricane'

'Spinner,' 'Spumonti,' and 'Rosa Spumonti' (Elliot)

Emma Elliot selected three very nice *S. arachnoideum* seedlings that are extensively webbed and very vigorous growers. Both of the "spumontis" form nice clumps rapidly and have an almost frothy look. 'Rosa Spumonti' has a touch more red than 'Spumonti,' but they are otherwise very similar. 'Spinner' is such a great name for a cobweb—I wish I had thought of it! It is a very vigorous cobweb cultivar that makes mounds quickly. It also makes some of the most symmetrically beautiful cobwebs of any cultivar.

'Poco Loco' (Mylin)

This cultivar is a bit loco! Normally, cobwebs have a bit of red on the outer leaves. In 'Poco Loco,' the red is quite variable, occurring as blots or splashes on the leaf, rather than an even suffusion. No two rosettes are exactly alike, and it makes a lovely clump that almost looks as though you have taken a paint brush with red paint and shot it over the clump of green cobwebbed rosettes. How cool is that?

Fig. 4-35. 'Spinner'

Fig. 4-37. 'Denise's Cobweb'

'Denise's Cobweb' (Drown-Warner)

This was one of Pat's first seedlings, and it is named for her sister, Denise. This is a rather typical *S. arachnoideum*, except that the stolons are more substantial than in most cobweb types and fewer offsets are produced, forming a more open clump. In addition, this cultivar produces fasciated rosettes with great regularity, and the fasciated forms are rather neat, not messy. Seedlings from this plant often inherit this same tendency.

Fig. 4-36. 'Poco Loco'

TUFTED TYPES

This is perhaps my favorite category of *Sempervivum* cultivars, as they combine the neat clump habit of *S. arachnoideum* with the colors, patterns, and larger sizes of the other cultivars. Instead of a full cobweb, the hairs on most of these hybrids are restricted to tufts of hair that do not usually coalesce into a full cobweb. In addition, many of these hybrids have inherited the very pretty rose-pink flowers from *S. arachnoideum* and the shorter stalks that look more proportionate in a clump. They tend to be less fertile than other groups, and some are nearly sterile. They also tend to increase very well and are very hardy.

'Aross' (Zonneveld)

A very distinctive hybrid. *S. ossetiense* is a green with a strong flush of red on the top of all the leaves and excessively long stolons; the cross with *S. arachnoideum* was just the right combination to shorten the stolons and make a pretty plum red rosette with contrasted white tufts of hair on each long-pointed leaf tip. A great combination! Although this is a rather wide cross, 'Aross' is fertile and gives very interesting seedlings.

'Alpha' and 'Beta' (Arends)

These two hybrids were the first planned crosses between *S. arachnoideum* and *S. tectorum*, and gave two very nice hybrids. 'Alpha' is an olive green rosette lightly flushed red and with very prominent fuzzy tips to the leaf. 'Beta' is a bit smaller rosette with much more red leaves that contrast with the strong tufts on each leaf. Neither of these hybrids is very fertile, perhaps indicating a triploid hybrid.

'Agnes' (Smits)

For a tufted type this is quite large, and the leaves have lots of hairs. The leaves are pale green heavily flushed with pink to red in the spring, and the color lasts fairly well into the summer. One of my favorites of the tufted types, and giving some very interesting seedlings in my effort to produce very large cobwebs.

'Frodo' (Bronow)

Betty Bronow did an inspired cross of 'Beta' X *S. arachnoideum* 'Kappa' to come up with this much fuzzier version of 'Beta.' Long silky plumes of hair occur at the tip of each leaf, and the rosette is a rich burgundy red that contrasts with the white tufts of hair. Makes a very neat mound. This is one of Betty's hybrids named for characters in the *Lord of the Rings* and is my favorite of Betty's hybrids.

'Green Ice' (Wills)

This cultivar really does look icy. The very light green rosettes are finely hairy and have terminal tufts of hair at the tip of each leaf, sometimes forming the most rudimentary of cobwebs. Makes neat clumps.

'Koko Flanel' (Smits)

What an interesting rosette. The leaves of this cultivar are short and sharply pointed, but the rosette has so many leaves it makes for a very full effect, especially because the symmetry of the rosette is so precise. The greyish leaf almost appears frosted, as the tufts on each coalesce in the center, almost like a full cobweb.

◄ **Fig. 4-38.** 'Green Ice'

➤ **Fig. 4-39.** 'Koko Flanel'

'Black Mini' (Ford)

I would not call this cultivar either black or mini, but it is a really nice semp. A medium-sized olive green semp that flushes a fairly dark red purple in spring. The leaves have prominent cilia along the leaf edge and a small tuft of hairs at the leaf tip.

'Zilver Moon' (Smits)

A very bright little rosette of sort of silvery green with prominent tufts of hair on each leaf. The older leaves are flushed a lovely shade of rose pink. Makes a very neat clump and is a good grower. This looks especially good near dark stones or brickwork.

'Bunny Girl' (Robertson)

This one just screams *cute*. A very hairy and exceedingly symmetrical medium small rosette of a sort of silvery green, sometimes flushed pink. One of my favorites of the tufted types. The bloomstalks on this are short, so you can leave them to complement the silvery rosettes. It is not too fertile, but what seedlings I have raised are very interesting.

'Pacific Spring Frost' (Gossett)

I *love* this plant. Such a cool plant, with a sort of pastel plum velvety leaves with prominent tufts of hair. The rosettes are medium-sized and have fairly broad leaves for a tufted type. The rosettes fade some, but remain attractive year round. The flowers on this plant are some of the biggest I have seen on a *Sempervivum* and are an attractive shade of pink. This plant has it all. I have used this quite a bit in crosses this year, as it has such an unusual combination of characters and I am anxiously waiting for the results.

'Ginnie's Delight' (Hallauer, but named by Payne)

This plant was originally distributed as simply #10 from Hallauer's Nursery in Webster, New York. Helen lamented that such a pretty plant did not sell well, but with the name #10 few customers were interested. She then renamed the plant 'Ginnie's Delight' and sales increased a good bit. This cultivar has medium-sized deep rose red leaves that are fringed and tufted with hairs, with this forming a congested mass in the center of the rosette. A very easy increaser.

'Raspberry Ice' and 'Silver Thaw' (Colvin)

Years ago, I started a round robin letter system that circulated among a core group of *Sempervivum* experts so as to maintain contact, long before there was an internet. Mina Colvin was a member of that group, and she circulated a slide of a group of seedlings from open-pollinated *S. arachnoideum* var. 'Tomentosum.' When I saw the slide, I told Mina she needed to save two seedlings that were obviously crosses to non-cobwebs. These two seedlings were later named 'Raspberry Ice' and 'Silver Thaw.' 'Raspberry Ice' is a great raspberry rose-colored rosette with prominent fuzz at the tip of each leaf. This will grow a bit bigger than its sister seedling. It won a Silver Rosette from the Sempervivum Society and is a most worthy plant. 'Silver Thaw' is sort of silvery grey with very prominent tufts of hair on each leaf, sometimes making the tiniest of cobwebs. The clump effect of 'Silver Thaw' is outstanding, as it makes very compact clumps and quickly fills in for plants that have bloomed. Neither plant is too fertile, but the seedlings are interesting. I wish I knew whom their pollen parent was.

'Icicle' (Skrocki)

Toward the end of his hybridizing career, Ed concentrated on developing more unusual cobwebs and tufted types. This is one of his most outstanding efforts in this group of plants. A very good deep red with leaves just dripping with heavy tufts of hair at the end of each leaf. The red color of the leaves and the white tufts of hair make for an outstanding contrast.

'Fluffy Fluke' (Skrocki)

In one of Ed Skrocki's interviews (*SempWorld* 1993), he proclaimed 'Fluffy Fluke' to be his favorite plant. It is a fine one, and has lots of fuzz and hair, making for a very fluffy-appearing rosette of silvery green with pink tints. This is a really interesting parent, giving seedlings with a wide range of colors and all sorts of variations in the extent of cobwebbing.

'Shirley's Joy' (Moore)

I remember when I first received this plant as a kid in Massachusetts. My mom was named Shirley, and this quickly became her favorite. It is still a very good plant. An obvious hybrid of *S. arachnoideum* and *S. marmoreum*, it has smooth leaves of green that are strongly flushed a pinkish rose at the leaf tips. The webbing is fairly heavy, and this can sometimes cause a problem in damp winters. Not overly fertile; I have only been able to grow just a handful of seedlings from it, and they too closely resemble their mother.

'Ann Christy' (Smits)

This is one of the larger tufted type plants, and with a little less obvious amount of hair tufts than many. An olive green rosette with hints of red that are more obvious in the spring. The shape is very distinctive, as the leaves are short and wide, and show a lot of curves that intersect to the shape of the rosette. A good grower and increaser. Plant this where you can observe the unusual leaf shapes. Ed Skrocki's 'Ohioan' is a bit similar, but does not produce the curved leaves quite as often as 'Ann Christy' does.

'St. Cloud' (Skrocki)

This plant has nearly a full cobweb, but the size and shape of the rosette indicates some non-cobweb blood somewhere in the pedigree. A very neat light green plant with a rather full cobweb and a low rosette that increases a bit more slowly than some other cobwebs and produces more spaced out rosettes on longer stolons, leading to less crowding in the clump.

'Deep Fire' (Skrocki)

When this cultivar is at its peak color it is *brilliant*. A really intense red. A neat medium-sized rosette with many rather thin leaves and tiny tufts of hair at the leaf tip. I have not had luck getting seedlings from this cultivar and not for lack of trying!

'Pacific Feather Power' (Gossett)

A very cool little semp. This is a great maroon red in spring with *lots* of fur and elaborate tufts of hair. It does look feathery. Has nice rose-pink flowers on rather short bloomstalks. A good increaser and a healthy plant.

'Pacific Sparkler' (Gossett)

This is such a neat and tidy little cultivar. The rosettes have small but many leaves, each with a tuft of hair at the tip of the leaves, and the rosettes are very symmetrical, enhancing this "neat" look. The color is redder in the spring and fades to an olive green by midsummer.

'Spring Mist' (Drown-Warner)

This was a volunteer seedling in Pat's garden, but may be related to 'Kanno's Cobweb' or 'Denise's Cobweb.' It is sort of a pastel lavender rosette of medium/small size with a strong tuft on each leaf tip. 'Spring Mist' makes very neat clumps, the bloomstalks are short, and the flowers a pleasing rose.

'Sweet Litschi' (Geiger)

What a cool little plant this is! First, it is a brilliant shade of rose red. The very narrow but numerous leaves are sort of ciliated and have a tiny tuft of hair at the tip of each leaf. Generally small semps are not my thing but I *love* this one.

Fig. 4-40. 'Sweet Litschi'

UNUSUAL FORMS

Teratological forms of *Sempervivum* are actually rather rare, although members of the Crassulaceae are known for their unusual forms (White 1948; Iliev and Kitin 2011). These include fasciated forms (crests), in which the normal meristematic tissues are organized along a line, rather than a dome; monstrose forms, which have highly thickened leaves; and quilled cultivars, in which the edges of the leaves curl under and are fused, making for a tube of lamina rather than a normal bifacial leaf. Praegar (1932) described fasciated forms of *S. arachnoideum*, *S. grandiflorum*, and *S. montanum* in the wild and *S. tectorum* in cultivation. The unusual forms actually include representatives from other groups, but the following have either asymmetrical rosettes or some other malformations of the leaf that give the rosette an unusual character. Some consider these plants ugly, or at best "conversation pieces." I have always liked them, but you may not want a yard of these. Rather, a few sprinkled here and there should be treated as surprises among a sea of more normal forms.

There is some controversy as to what causes these unusual forms. Some are clearly a sort of mutation that affects either the organization of the shoot apical meristem or the ability of the leaf primordia to form a normal bifacial leaf. In other members of the Crassulaceae, there has been documentation of phytoplasmas—bacteria that cause abnormal growth— generally resulting in Witch's broom or fasciated types of growth patterns (Dewir et al. 2015). No phytoplasmas have as yet been demonstrated in *Sempervivum*, nor has there been any evidence that growing crested or monstrose forms next to normal rosettes will cause similar abnormal formations in their neighbors. It might be interesting to try grinding leaves of teratological forms and applying the paste to rosettes of normal cultivar to see if the fasciate trait can be transferred (Smith 1971).

Many cultivars will produce a fasciate rosette on occasion. Some cultivars have much more of a tendency to do this than others. Some, such as 'Denise's Cobweb,' will produce them each season and pass on this tendency to their seedlings. In general, the offsets from fasciated plants also tend to be fasciated. The following cultivars are ones that do it most consistently.

'Weirdo' (Vaughn)

This plant was unusual from day one. When it appeared as a seedling, it had no true center to the rosette and tiny offsets began shooting out of the center of the rosette on minute stolons, splitting the crown. It was immediately dubbed 'Weirdo,' and has continued this strange behavior through many millions of vegetative divisions. I had thought the seedlings were from 'Emerald Spring' X self (Vaughn and Nixon 1972), but I think I might have inadvertently carried pollen from a non-*Jovibarba* type, as in those days I did not clean my tweezers between pollinations and probably carried over some pollen. In that batch of seedlings there were six roller types similar to 'Emerald Spring' and two like 'Weirdo.' Hatch (1984) found that crosses between *Jovibarba* types and non-*Jovibarba* types gave plants similar to 'Weirdo' in support of this idea. Moreover, the flowers on 'Weirdo' are produced rarely, and are of an unusual shade of greenish white (more like a roller type) with very malformed parts, including fasciation of the stems and flowers. The flowers do not have the campanulate shape of a roller type.

'Fuzzy Wuzzy' (Vaughn)

If you like crests, this is the one for you. A tiny cobweb with virtually every rosette fasciated. The rosettes are very small and lightly tinged lavender. This is from a cross of 'Marietta' X 'Denise's Cobweb,' and inherited its ability to fasciate from the pollen parent, which also fasciates with frequency, although not as much as its offspring. The cobweb is rather sparse and recalls the line of the song and nursery rhyme (author unknown):

Fuzzy Wuzzy was a bear;
Fuzzy Wuzzy had no hair!
Fuzzy Wuzzy wasn't fuzzy, wuz he?

'Fuzzy Wuzzy' makes tiny clumps that are like rounded balls. I have never seen it bloom. 'Just Plain Crazy' (Vaughn) is a bigger plant with similar sorts of fasciated and irregular rosettes.

'Mad Hatter' (Vaughn)

In my effort to make a bigger version of 'Fuzzy Wuzzy,' I crossed 'Denise's Cobweb' with 'Killer.' I was hoping for a big red tufted type with fasciation. I got part of my wish, as 'Mad Hatter' makes bigger rosettes and huge crests. A very fun and odd plant for the collector.

◄ **Fig. 4-41.** 'Fuzzy Wuzzy'

▼ **Fig. 4-42.** 'Mad Hatter'

◄ **Fig. 4-43.** 'Oddity'

'Oddity' (MacPherson)

Sandy MacPherson discovered this "quilled" leaf form in a cultivar known as 'Albidum,' which is probably a selection of *S. tectorum*. Unlike normal semp leaves, the leaves of 'Oddity' appear to be bent back on to themselves like a cannoli, sometimes forming a thickened leaf, but most of the leaves form a tube, with the lamina of the leaf surrounding this cavity. The leaves are green with a conspicuous purple tip that accentuates the quilled tip. 'Oddity' is likely a chimera—a plant made up of genetically different tissues—as bud sports look like the typical 'Albidum.' Blooms appear infrequently and are very poorly fertile. Lynn Smith has observed two sorts of bloomstalks in her clumps of 'Oddity,' with one being more extreme than the other, indicating there may be various amounts/combinations of mutant tissue in any given rosette. Fertility of these appears to be limited, and none of the seedlings are quilled at present. 'Oddity' won a Bronze Rosette from the Sempervivum Society.

'Fame Monstrose'

This plant is frustrating! When it is in the monstrose phase, it is one of my favorite cultivars. 'Fame' itself is a large plant, and this sport has leaves that are highly thickened, so the brilliant red leaf bases seem even more brilliant. However, 'Fame Monstrose' often appears the same as 'Fame.' Conversely, a clump will be showing mainly normal rosettes and several obvious monstrose forms appear. This is still one that you should grow, despite its shortcomings. The monstrose rosettes are really cool, and even the normal ones are attractive.

Fig. 4-44. 'Fame Monstrose'

Shirley Rempel found this sport in a row of the red velvet cultivar 'Cleveland Morgan' and separated it out as something special. 'Whirligigs' include any sort of toy or lawn ornament, such as a pinwheel or lawn ornament, that becomes animated in the wind. The semp cultivar has that same sort of feeling, as the rosettes have odd bits that are more extended than the remainder of the rosette, and the rosette often produces crown divisions like a *heuffelii*. This cultivar was awarded an Award of Merit by the Sempervivum Society.

'Grigg's Surprise' (a.k.a. S. calcareum 'Monstrosum')

'Grigg's Surprise' was the first of these quilled semps to be described. It was so unlike any *Sempervivum* previously seen that it was actually classified as a species from other succulent genera (Smith 1971). Only when a plant bloomed was it possible to classify this plant as a *Sempervivum*. Unlike 'Oddity,' the tubular leaves of 'Grigg's Surprise' are closed right to the tip, so there is no hollow area, just a highly thickened, tubular leaf. Being a sport of *S. calcareum*, it closely resembles the species in leaf color and pattern, and also in rarely flowering in cultivation. Makes a neat, slow-growing clump.

Fig. 4-45. 'Grigg's Surprise'

HEUFFELII CULTIVARS

These are becoming my favorites, and it is amazing that a single species could exhibit such variety. Most of these are fairly easy to grow and rarely, if ever, require division and replanting. If a clump gets large occasionally it will naturally break into pieces, but otherwise you can just leave them in place if you grow them in a garden situation. Colors range from greens, quite strong yellows, and reds to purples. The flowers come on relatively short stalks and have cream to yellow flowers. On the red cultivars, the contrast between the pale flowers and the red rosettes is especially nice. The *heuffelii* types can bloom, but the clump quickly fills into the void created by the blooming rosette. The type plant for *S. heuffelii* was a pubescent one, but the majority of selections are glabrous.

— GREEN OR MOSTLY GREEN —

'Henri Correvon' (Correvon)

This plant, or something very similar, was first distributed in the US as 'Pallasii' (and reportedly came from Correvon's nursery as such), and was one of the hot plants when I was a kid in Massachusetts in the '70s. My plant came from Bill Newhard in Pennsylvania. It became obvious that this matched a form distributed in Europe as 'Correvon's Form'; Peter Mitchell made the change to 'Henri Correvon' to separate it from other clones from Correvon nursery. 'Henri Correvon' is big and green with relatively upright leaves and prominent purple tips on each leaf. This is a rapid increaser for a crown divider.

'Sunny Side Up' (Nixon)

This is a big, vigorous plant that is an easy grower. If you have trouble growing *heuffelii* types then this is one you should try before giving up on the group. A bright green rosette with purple tips to the leaves. Bigger and more upright than most cultivars. Bill Nixon repudiated this cultivar toward the end of his career, but as a garden plant it is still wonderful. Similar to his 'Sundancer,' but a bigger plant as it grows for me in Oregon. Although the pedigree of this plant is unknown, it may be related to 'Pallasii' or 'Henri Correvon.'

Fig. 4-46. 'Sunny Side Up'

'Springael's Choice' (Springael)

This is one of the largest of the *heuffelii* cultivars and the rosette lies fairly flat to the ground. A bright green with very prominent and bright purple tips to the leaves. I agree with the hybridizer, this is one I would choose, too!

'Apache' (named by Payne, but not her hybrid)

When I was growing up, we had several *heuffelii* hybrids that were listed by a number alone; this was designated "#1." Helen gave this one the cultivar name 'Apache.' It is a good one. A big plant with wide green leaves and very dark purple tips that make for a good contrast. Unlike most, this one is finely pubescent.

'Jade' (Ford)

Surprisingly all green with no purple influence *heuffelii* types are fairly rare. This is one of the good ones, a very clear shade. Nicely formed and good to use in beds to contrast with red or purple types.

'Faith' (Mylin)

The plant circulating under this name in the US is a rather large sort of pastel green with light brown tips, with a glaucous coating that gives it a blue effect. It is a very good grower and a nice contrast to the red cultivars. The plant listed in Europe is a small red one. My plant came directly from Don, so I am assuming it is the correct one.

— GOLD AND ORANGE —

In the *S. heuffelii* cultivars there are some amazingly good gold to orange rosettes. These have their optimum color in the early spring and then gradually green. These are termed "virescent," as they start out pale and gradually turn green. Climate and the speed at which temperatures warm in the spring greatly influence how long the plant stays in the gold or orange phase. Here in the Pacific Northwest, with our prolonged spring, the colors last up to several months. In Massachusetts it was much less, sometimes weeks. A new group of cultivars in this group have recently been introduced in Europe from the hand of the talented hybridizer Schara. These all have "cheese" somewhere in their name and are either fully yellow or yellow with reddish tips. This group is from open pollinated seed of 'Gold Bug' and 'Orange Tip,' and the most vigorous and colorful seedlings were selected after several years of rigorous selection. Watch for these as they reach the American market.

'Xanthoheuff' (Skrocki)

This was the start of the yellow cultivars. At first Ed just called it the 'Yellow Form,' but then coined the named 'Xanthoheuff.' The rosette starts out in spring as a very bright yellow, so yellow you fear it does not have enough chlorophyll to live. Gradually the rosettes turn a soft lime green, and in the fall develop a bit of reddish backs to the leaves. This is a tricky plant. It can rot, or if the sun is too hot too early in the year it can be wounded. I grow mine in sharply drained soil and with gravel all around the neck of the plant. It is worth the effort.

'Gold Bug' (Skrocki)

Wow, this one is *bright*! Although 'Xanthoheuff' is a bright yellow, the leaves of 'Gold Bug' have prominent red tips that really set the yellow color off beautifully. 'Gold Bug' seems to be a better grower too and requires less pampering to keep it alive. This is one of my *must haves*.

'Lemon Sky' (Skrocki)

This is what Ed considered his improvement on his classic 'Xanthoheuff.' It is a brighter sort of lemon-gold. The plant is compact in the spring, but as the leaves turn green they expand, making for a more upright rosette. This is one that is *very* sensitive to growing conditions. The best advice is to grow this plant in at least some shade, otherwise the leaves burn and the plant can die. All three of the Skrocki yellow *heuffelii* cultivars are from the seed of a plant then known as 'Kopaonikense' that originally came from Correvon's nursery. It was green, but obviously carried genes for gold plants.

'Orange Tip' (Zonneveld)

'Orange Tip' might be the most vigorous of the "yellow" *heuffelii* cultivars. It is a somewhat less bright yellow than 'Gold Bug,' but the leaf tips are an amazing orange-red that set the whole rosette on fire. The rosettes are medium small, but they increase at a fairly good rate, making small clumps. In Oregon, this keeps its color for the longest of any of the yellow

Fig. 4-47. 'Orange Tip'

heuffelii cultivars. It is proving to be a very interesting parent, based on Schara's 'Cheese' series and seedlings of my own.

— RED OR PREDOMINANTLY RED —

'Vesta' (Zonneveld)

This is one of my favorite *heuffelii* cultivars. The shape is very distinctive: the rosettes are flat, and the many leaves are arranged in a very precise and symmetrical matter. This pattern is further enhanced by the very precise green edging to the red-purple leaves, giving a sort of pinwheel effect. 'Vesta' is a seedling from open pollinated seed of the *S. heuffelii* from Vihren.

'Torrid Zone' (Nixon)

This was a major breakthrough in the color of the *heuffelii* cultivars, as it had such bright red color. The waxy surface to the leaf makes this color glow even more. This cultivar is from seed of 'Giuseppi Spiny' with 'Henri Correvon' as the possible pollen parent. A good grower and one that retains its color for much of the season.

'Hot Lips' (Nixon)

This was another major breakthrough in color in the *heuffelii* cultivars like 'Torrid Zone,' but in this case, along with bright red and persistent coloration, the leaves have exceptional width and lie very flat. 'Hot Lips' is a seedling of 'Chocoleto.'

'Bloodstone' (Nixon)

This was Bill's pick of his red cultivars and it is a fine one. 'Bloodstone' has very dark red leaves and incredibly good color persistence. There is rarely a time of year when the rosettes are not this deep, very intense rose red shade. This one grows only to a medium size for me, although I have seen it grow larger for others.

'Inferno' (Nixon)

This is the fourth of the quartet of Nixon red *heuffelii* cultivars. 'Inferno' is the biggest of the three and a very solid brilliant red. This is my pick of the four, although all are well worth growing. 'Inferno' is a seedling from 'Tan.'

'Bros' (Ford)

This is one of my favorite red *heuffelii* cultivars, as it has an amazingly bright red color that is intense and a color that lasts all seasons. May be the best of all of David Ford's many hybrids. This is one that has especially great contrast between the yellow flowers and the bright red stalks. Seedlings from 'Bros' have so far been disappointing, but I am still trying, as it is such a beautiful cultivar.

Fig. 4-48. 'Bros'

'Be Mine' (Wills)

A very intense dark red rosette. The rosettes are quite small and make an incredibly neat clump. When the plant blooms, the contrast between the red rosettes, stalk foliage, and yellow flowers is striking. Certainly my favorite smaller *heuffelii*.

'Mink' (Ford)

This one grows fairly small for me and forms a very compact clump of sort of red-purple leaves. The short leaves are quite pointed, and the plant lies fairly flat to the ground. Finely hairy. The color lasts very well throughout the season.

'Clown' (Smits)

This cultivar really is a clown! I am not sure whether this is a green cultivar with splashes of red throughout or a red cultivar with splashes of green. Either way it is *very* unique. The only other cultivar at all similar to this pattern is the cobweb cultivar 'Poco Loco.' This has now been imported to the US, so we hope it will be offered soon by US nurseries. Based on early growth of the plant here it appears to be a larger than normal rosette with very wide leaves.

Fig. 4-49. 'Clown'

'Jovi King' (Versteeg)

There are times when this cultivar earns its title as "king." It can have incredibly bright red leaves, but there are other times when it is pretty, although not as flashy green, with the upper third of the leaf a dark red. This is one I hope to use as a parent to get one fixed in the incredibly bright red mode. Seems to be a good increaser.

Somehow I expected this cultivar to be yellow, not red, but it is a lovely red. Sort of red purple with a wire rim of green to the leaf that sets off the color.

— BROWN TO COPPER —

'Copper King' (Ford)

This cultivar can be variable in color, but it is always a nice color, varying from olive green, to dark brown, to nearly black. A very compact form. The leaves are lined with tiny cilia that set off the dark colors of the leaf.

'Nannette' (Nixon)

Bill Nixon considered this one of his best efforts and he named it for his mother. This is quite a small *heuffelii*, and it has an unusual mix of colors (browns, violet, and red), generally with a lighter, almost olive green edge to each leaf.

'Tuxedo' (Ford)

This is an incredible changeable rosette: from a golden brown with green leaf bases in the spring, it transforms into a near black in the fall. All of the color guises of this plant are pretty. It is an Award of Merit winner of the Sempervivum Society.

'Tan' (Fearnley)

I would not call the color of this cultivar tan per se, but it is a red-brown, with the base of the leaves a bright lime green that contrasts nicely with the upper portions of the leaf. Not a fast grower, but a good, solid plant. Seedlings from this plant even from self-pollination give a wide variety of colors.

'Limelight' (Geiger)

I expected this cultivar to be a lime green by its name (the *S. calcareum* form is a very distinctive lime green), and it does have bits of lime color, but there are also swirls of brown and lavender that go through the rosette, so that the landscape color is sort of a café au lait. This has given very interesting seedlings, many with swirls of color.

ROLLER HYBRIDS

There have been few deliberate crosses between the subspecies or forms of *S. globiferum*, although there are a number of wild accessions of these species and its forms that offer unique colors or forms. Many of the collected forms of the rollers are wonderful garden plants and offer colors not found in any of the hybrids.

'Emerald Spring' (Vaughn)

This was one of my first crosses, using the form of *S. globiferum ssp. hirtum* known as 'Histoni' as the pod parent and a large selection of *S. globiferum ssp. globiferum* as the pollen parent. 'Emerald Spring' was the spikiest and brightly colored, with light green with tones of yellow, red, and purple depending on the time of year and exposure. Like all roller types, this makes offsets on thin stolons which quickly fall and root around the mother rosette. A sister seedling named 'Emerald Fountain,' which had more the shape of the pollen parent, was not marketed, although it was distributed to a few friends.

'Hedgehog' (MacPherson)

'Hedgehog' has rather narrow, sharply pointed leaves and many of them, making for a very full rosette. The rosettes are a good dark green and are marked on the back side of the leaves with a deep mahogany. Unlike 'Emerald Spring,' 'Hedgehog' has very incurved leaves.

'Madame Lorene' (Thomas)

Leo and Betty Thomas ran Arcady Gardens in Medford, Oregon, for many years and specialized in *Sempervivum*. 'Madame Lorene' is a medium-sized roller type with green, incurved rosettes and prominent red leaf backs.

'Limette' and 'Arctic Fire' (Thomas)

There has been a long hiatus in the production of new and exciting roller type plants. These two have just reached the US, but it is hoped they will be available commercially soon here. Both are big advancements in color in this group. 'Limette' is, as the name suggests, a cool lime green. Unlike others in this color range, 'Limette' appears to be a good plant that increases readily. 'Arctic Fire' has a more traditional coloring of green with red on the backs of the leaves, but the red is extremely bright, beyond fire engine red. Both seem to be very good growers.

'Jowan' (Zonneveld)

Ben Zonneveld made a number of crosses between the roller types and *S. heuffelii* cultivars. These hybrids are now known collectively as *S. x nixonii* to honor C. William Nixon, founder of the Sempervivum Fancier's Association. All of these hybrids are sterile or nearly so. 'Jowan' is my pick of these types of hybrids. In this cross the *S. heuffelii* parent was 'Bronze Ingot,' and this gave 'Jowan' a distinctive red-brown color in the spring that transforms to lime with traces of red. The methods of increase are sort of intermediate between the rollers and *S. heuffelii*—a form of crown division—but they divide much easier than those from pure *S. heuffelii* breeding.

REFERENCES

Bronow BZ (1986) "Sempervivum 'Butterbur.'" *Sempervivum Fancier's Association Newsletter* 7 (2): 9

Dewir YH, AF Omar, YH Hafez, ME El-Mahrouk, RY Mourad (2015) "Fasciation in *Crassula argentea*: molecular identification of phytoplasmas and associated antioxidative capacity." *Phytoparsitica doi:* 10.1007/s12600-015-0497-7

Hatch, L. C. (1984) "Vegetative anomalies in controlled intrageneric (Sempervivum x Sempervivum) and intergeneric (Sempervivum x Jovibarba) crosses." *Sempervivum Fanciers Association Newsletter* 10(2): 7–10

Iliev I, P Kitin (2011) "Origin, morphology, and anatomy of fasciation in plants cultured in vivo and in vitro." *Plant Growth Regul* 63: 115–129

Praegar LR (1932) *An Account of the Sempervivum Group.* The Royal Horticultural Society. London, UK

Smith M (1971) "Freak Sempervivums." *Sempervivum Society J* 1971 (4): 2-7

Vaughn KC, CW Nixon (1972) "An unexplained lack of symmetry, possibly hereditary, in the Sempervivum group." *Sempervivum Society J* 1972 (3): 6

White OE (1948) "Fasciation." *Bot Rev* 14: 319-358

CHAPTER 5

METHODS OF PROPAGATION

To us old-timers working with semps, the thought of being instructed how to propagate semps seems pretty silly, as they are about the easiest plants on the planet to propagate. However, there are a few tricks that will improve your success. The propagation of S. *heuffelii* is a much trickier issue, though, and will require more explanation to achieve maximum success.

PROPAGATION FROM OFFSETS

A mature semp rosette will generally send out a number of offsets on stolons at some point during the growing season. The cobweb types tend to produce offsets in two flushes, and in the case of the roller types, the production of offsets can continue throughout the entire season.

For the majority of semps, the daughter rosettes occur at the end of fairly stout stolons that arise from areas between the outermost (oldest) leaves of the mother rosette. As the daughter rosette at the end of the rosette begins to mature, a number of small roots develop underneath the daughter rosette. At this point, the offset may be detached from the mother rosette and grown on its own. Some gardeners keep a bit of the stolon attached and poke the stolon into the ground to help support the new plant. There appears to be no great advantage to leaving this bit of stolon attached and it can rot. If the stolon is still turgid I will leave a small piece, no more than ½ in. for a medium-large rosette. A weak fertilizer treatment, such as those used for transplanting, will give the young plant a good start in its new location. Young plants require a bit more moisture until the plant has produced roots sufficient to support their growth. If the daughter rosette is transplanted during warmer periods of the summer, covering the plant with a bit of shade, such as a berry basket, is helpful, giving the plant a bit less stress. Alternately, offsets removed from the mother rosette may be potted up and kept in the shade until new growth is noted. After the plant is well-rooted the potted offset can be safely moved to a permanent spot in the garden.

With the cobweb types, the increases are so small and the rate of increase is so fast, I would never sever the small daughter rosettes; rather, I would leave them attached to the mother until they are firmly rooted. A clump of cobweb rosettes is probably best divided into small clumps of three to four rosettes rather than dividing them into single rosettes, as they are so small.

The roller type semps will be even easier, as most of the offsets will have fallen from the mother rosette by the time you even think about trying to propagate them. The stolon on the rollers is very thin and ephemeral. Unlike the offsets on most semp species, the ones on the rollers are produced closer to the growing tip, whereas in the normal semps the stolons are produced close to the ground level. As soon as the rosette develops sufficient weight and size the entire offset detaches and rolls to a new spot. In the wild, this serves the purpose of distributing propagules of a clone for a fairly great distance. This would be even more exacerbated by the relatively mountainous situations of most of these plants, so gravity could move the offset a good distance. Despite the lack of roots of these rolling offsets, the plants rapidly make roots in their new situation and quickly establish a new colony. The strategy of producing numerous, highly mobile offsets compensates in many ways for the relatively low seed production of the roller types compared to other types of semps. For example, I have never known S. *globiferum ssp. arenarium* to bloom in Oregon in the six years it has been in my garden, and my cultivar 'Emerald Spring' has only bloomed once with its very snakey bloomstalk.

Fig. 5-1. A roller seedling of the author's producing numerous offsets on very thin stolons that detach quickly.

As easy as these other groups are in propagation, the many cultivars of S. *heuffelii* are a totally different matter. When the S. *heuffelii* rosette matures to a certain size, the crown splits in from two to seven smaller crowns, with each of the resulting meristems. In closer observations of cross sections cut through a dividing meristem, the crown is apparently not dividing, but actually producing very short, thick stolons (Zonneveld 1981). This growth habit leads to the production of a plant with a fairly large woody crown beneath the cluster of rosettes. Because no stolons with offsets nor rolling offsets are produced, a different method must be used to propagate these plants. I find it easiest to sort of cheat Mother Nature a bit. After the multiheaded rosettes have developed some size, with each of the daughter rosettes from one-third to one-quarter the size of a mature rosette, I take a very sharp knife and cut down through the rosette, making an incision that goes through the rosette and down into the crown. By leaving the plant in the ground, I find that each severed rosette starts to grow on its own more quickly than on divisions which have not been severed. By the end of the season, the rosettes are fully developed, but are detached from their neighbor. I can then share the results with friends or start new colonies of that cultivar in my garden. Not all *heuffelii* cultivars are created equal in terms of being propagated in this manner. You may want to experiment with this technique on a less choice cultivar, or with one in which you have many spare divisions. If all of this scares you to death, you can leave the clump for several years. After the clump has produced flowering rosettes, the remaining rosettes appear to be much more easily separated just by pulling apart the rosettes in the clump and replanting each piece.

The method that most of us were trained to do is one that Helen Payne used and is described in her book (Payne 1972). Dig up the entire clump of the *heuffelii* cultivar, take a very sharp knife, and cut out each of the rosettes, making sure that each rosette has a portion of the thick crown. Helen then treated with a rooting hormone powder and a fungicide (I think she used Arasan, but she does not specify in her book), then let the cut ends dry in the shade. Most of us have found that the treatments are not necessary as long as the cut surfaces are allowed to dry before replanting. I have not tried this, but others have cut the rosettes in half and each of the pieces will also grow. They will not look perfect for a season, but you will have increased your stock of the plant a great deal.

▶ ▲ ◀ **Figs. 5-2, 5-3, and 5-4.** Steps in the division of an *S. heuffelii* cultivar. A rosette is removed from the soil, the soil washed away, and a stout knife used to cut the rosettes in the clump apart. Rosettes are allowed to dry so that the wounded tissue re-heals.

ACCELERATED OFFSET PRODUCTION

Plants regulate their growth via a number of plant hormones that influence the rate of cell division, cell elongation, and maturation. Endogenously-applied hormones can markedly affect plant growth. Used judiciously, these can be applied to plants to markedly improve the amount of increase.

Configure,® or N-(phenylmethyl)-1H-purine-6-amine is a synthetic plant hormone that is used to increase compact habit in container plants, and in the case of semps, greatly increases the number of stolons that will produce. Check the label for proper concentrations. Treatment with Configure® can increase the number of new offsets from a crown by twenty to one-hundredfold and can be done at multiple times in the season. Soon a cultivar can be increased to hundreds and thousands of plants. Although this is of more interest to those involved in commercial operations, if you would like to create huge numbers of a given cultivar for a ground cover, or to use in local plant sales, this is something you might want to consider.

PROPAGATION FROM LEAVES

Members of the Crassulaceae are renowned for their ability to grow new plants from virtually any part of the plant (Guo et al. 2014), although within the Crassulaceae there seem to be certain species that are more adept at making new plants than others. Semps have some of these abilities, but they are not as adept as plants like *Kalanchoe*, which is able to produce plantlets from the tiniest bits of tissue.

With semps, one technique that works with some success is to cleanly sever leaves with a sharp knife and then take the cut end and treat it with a commercial rooting hormone powder. The treated leaf is then placed in an upright position in moistened potting mix. Afterward, the leaves are maintained under very indirect light and watered sparingly until new growth is evident. I find a shaded patio ideal for this, but any spot where the leaves are not exposed to direct light and will only receive a bit of provided moisture will suffice.

Fig. 5-5. Leaf propagation.

The chances for rot are fairly great, but in several weeks there will often be small roots and a small rosette will become more obvious. Although this method is not utilized much, it may be helpful in propagating some of the slower cultivars and species. This technique might be useful on *S. wulfenii* or slow cultivars such as 'Grunrand' or 'Junimond' that are very slow propagators. I can't think of a person doing this with any roller, but I can't see why it would not work.

TISSUE CULTURE

Tissue culture is the technique of taking a sample of a plant and growing it in a sterile medium. Because whole plants can be obtained from very tiny bits of initial tissue, tissue culture has the advantage of rapidly upscaling the number of plants that would be available. Rare cultivars could be produced en masse so they would be more available to the public. Semps have rather high contents of natural products that are of pharmacological interest, and growing the plants under sterile conditions would allow for extraction of the compounds without decimating the plants. The tannins and other phenolic compounds found at high concentrations in semps have shown promising antimicrobial and anticancer uses, making semps a plant of interest.

Each plant species responds in tissue culture to a different set of growth media and hormone concentrations, and these must be determined empirically. Vantu (2010) was able to tissue culture S. *globiferum* from fragments of the rosette when grown on the classic Murashige-Skoog medium supplemented with cytokinin benzyl adenosine. Because rooting was inhibited on this medium, the addition of auxin was necessary to get reliable rooting of the rosettes. Although these techniques are beyond the scope of most home gardeners, there are labs that will culture plants. If you want thousands of plants of a very special cultivar this might be a plan.

SAVING A BLOOMING ROSETTE

Nothing is more discouraging than getting a new special cultivar and then having that rosette bloom. Because semps are monocarpic, this generally means the end. However, you can sometimes interrupt this process enough that the cultivar is not lost. From my experience, the earlier in the flowering cycle the better off you are in saving the rosette. Once you see the crown elongating, getting ready to bolt, simply decapitate the rosette by taking off the top inch or so of the stem, then wait. At this point the plant seems to do one of two things: in many cases, the plant will try to produce another bloomstalk. If that is so, you can try the same decapitation of the newly formed bloomstalk. In other cases, the crown will make from one to many small rosettes, usually along the remnants of the old stalk. Let these small plants develop and then detach them from the stem and pot up the plants in good potting soil in shade. Roots should develop on these small plants and you have saved the cultivar. On some occasions I have had all of these small rosettes also bolt, as the induction to the flowering state has triggered these plants to bloom. Plants that have been stressed are more likely to bloom without increase. For example, I had a bunch of plants that were delayed in customs for six weeks and they arrived nearly dead. A high percentage of the plants bloomed, although the dealer had included several rosettes, so that at least a few of each cultivar persisted. I wish I had potted up these plants rather than planting them in the garden. This is often a better way to handle plants to prevent this from occurring.

PROPAGATION BY SEED

Cultivars do not come true from seed, and even seed from species, if grown in the presence of other species or cultivars, are likely to be crossed rather than a pure species. However, growing semp plants from seed or hybridizing semps is a fun hobby. Details of these techniques and the ways to raise seedlings are described in the chapter on hybridizing.

REFERENCES

Guo J, L Hailiang, H Tangyang, C Xianghuan, D Xiling, J Zhu (2014) "Origin of asexual plantlets in three species of Crassulaceae." *Protoplasma* DOI 10.1007/s00709-014-0704-2

Payne HE (1972) *Plant Jewels of the High Country*. Pine Cone Pub. Medford, Oregon

Vantu S (2010) "In vitro multiplication of *Jovibarba sobolifera*. Anale Stintiflice ae Universitatii 'Alexandra Ion Cuza'" *Sectiunea Genetica si Biologie Moleculara* 11: 145-150

Zonneveld BJM (1981) "An analysis of the process of vegetative propagation in *Jovibarba heuffelii*." *Sempervivum Fanciers Association Newsletter* 7:13–16

CHAPTER 6

PESTS AND DISEASES

We are fortunate that semps are such easy and carefree plants. If your culture is good and you provide a relatively well-drained site for your plants, you may never experience any of these pests. It is good to know the early signs of these diseases and pests so they may be dealt with quickly before they become more widespread problems.

ANIMALS OF ALL SORTS

Insects

When I was growing semps as a kid in Massachusetts, I never noted any damage by insects in my plants, but growing them in other climates and conditions has shown that these can occasionally become a problem. In one of my beds in Oregon I had used potting soil, as the soil beneath was a hard-packed base of crushed concrete that was used to form a parking area. Instead of trying to work up this packed-down mess, I decided to ignore the soil and use the potting mix as the sole component to create a bed for the plants. In this bed alone I found two problems: vine weevils and root aphids (also called root mealybugs). Friends that only grow their plants in pots frequently find these, and inadvertently I had created a 20 ft. × 5 ft. pot! It is the grub of the vine weevil that does the most damage to the semp rosette. Weevil grubs are small and white. In response to light they seem to curl up. A first indication of their presence is that the rosette turns an unusual color and sometimes shows rotten outer leaves. Outer leaves will sometimes just dry out. If you lift up the rosette because of lack of roots, inspect the base of the plant and check for the presence of grubs. I just remove them and place the grubs on my patio as food for birds, as I very rarely find them. For a more effective control, both natural insecticides and biocontrol agents are useful. Careful inspection of rosette damage is useful if you have but a small infection. Root aphids or mealybugs are very tiny organisms, but they leave a very telltale sign of white powder in the soil around the root zone. Again, these seem to be a problem in potting soil, but not in real garden soil. The easiest solution is to remove the plants from infected areas, wash them thoroughly to remove any trace of the insects, and plant in fresh potting soil away from the area where the mealybugs have been found. This will allow the plant to form fresh roots in a mealybug-free environment. Watch the area where the mealybugs are found and treat the area with an insecticide. Some products containing rotenone—a natural insecticide—will help control the problem. In the South, every time I made a raised bed or filled a trough with soil this invited fire ants to invade the pots. Believe me, there is *no worse surprise* than encountering them in the garden. Fortunately, there are lots of good ant control treatments for the homeowner. In severe cases, many pest control services offer treatments that keep areas free of these extremely annoying pests. Ants can also bring aphids. I have never noted a severe invasion of these pests on semps; although occasional bloomstalks will have aphids, they are generally of little problem. With a garden with so many other plants that aphids adore, it is more likely they will find them before the semps.

Slugs and Snails

In the Pacific Northwest slugs are legion. We even have banana slugs that are up to six inches in length. Luckily semps are not their favorite plant, although in winter, where few other green plants are present, slugs will attack semps. The attack seems to be less extensive in beds where gravel mulch is used, perhaps because the rough edges of the stones make traversing it to attack the plants difficult. Addition of diatomaceous earth, which has very sharp edges, will also slow down slugs, and the treatment lasts for a full season. Several slug and snail baits are effective, including some with iron compounds rather than metaldehyde that are a bit more eco-friendly. Although for most plants the problems are worst in the spring, semps seem to be under attack more in winter and early spring. Accordingly, use of slug bait should be started much earlier in the season in beds that contain semps. More benign techniques include the time-honored use of beer. Low pans of beer placed near semps will attract slugs and they will drown in the beer. One caveat for those who also own cats—cats are also fans of beer, and you may have one very smashed cat using this technique!

Birds

For some reason, birds seem to be fascinated with semps. Jays in the Pacific Northwest are very interested and will pick at the rosettes, causing damage. Other species tend to lift up the entire rosette and capsize it. Whether they are hunting for insects or are somehow tasting the rosettes I am not sure. Although it is not attractive, bird netting hung over the bed, or simply spread on top of the rosettes, will greatly inhibit this activity. As detailed years ago in the *Sempervivum Society Journal*, a Dutch enthusiast ended up creating an Alpine house (cold greenhouse) for his semps because blackbirds would constantly destroy his plantings. I am glad I do not live where blackbirds are that prevalent.

Mammals

There are two different types of animal damage: actually eating the plants and disturbing flower beds. Deer and rabbits will occasionally eat portions of semps. Generally, it is only *one bite*, as they can find much more palatable things to eat. Semps have lots of malic acid and tannins that would leave a very acrid taste. I have also successfully used sprays on the leaves of the plants that dissuade deer and rabbits even more. It is fairly nasty to apply and smells bad, but does the job. In my garden, deer also decide that it is great fun to run through the beds, crushing semps as they go. Oddly enough, Lynn Smith's deer seem to stay out of her beds. Hers are a bit taller (two to three feet) than mine (eight inches), and that may prove to be more of a barrier to deer invading the beds. Chipmunks and squirrels seem to have the same perverse behavior as birds of digging up and moving rosettes, and seem to especially do this on newly planted rosettes. I have used landscape pins to fasten these small rosettes to the ground. Alternately, bird netting will also stop chipmunks and squirrels. In Oregon soils are alive with earthworms, and that proves to be a happy hunting ground not only for birds, but also for moles. These tunneling menaces can destroy a bed of semps in an evening, sinking the semps into the ground or covering them with soil from their tunnels. Semps are not amused by this treatment. I have tried everything from ultrasonic deterrents, mole pellets in

Fig. 6-1. Deer damage. The tips of the rosette are chewed away.

the holes, and a general spread to deter the entrance of moles. None of them was totally successful, but a local service that put down traps did a great job. It was pricey, but it worked!

ABIOTIC STRESSES

Hail

Hail is a problem for a plant that is mostly wide open and has very fleshy rosettes like semps. In spring 2016, a moderate to severe hailstorm hit my garden. Virtually every semp plant in the garden suffered some kind of damage. The damage was obvious in little pock marks on the leaves. In the case of the darker semps this was more obvious, as the anthocyanin-containing cells occur in the epidermal cells. When they are abraded the inner green tissue shows. The damage was less in a bed protected by a branch of a Douglas fir. Because hail is such a rare event protecting against it is difficult. If thunderstorms with large hail are predicted, quickly covering the beds with sheets or Reemay should prevent the worst damage. Even after the hail damage had occurred in my garden no plants were lost and most were fully recovered by fall.

Fig. 6-2. Hail damage is obvious as small dots where the anthocyanin-containing cells have been abraded by the hail.

Winter Rain

Because semps are plants of the high mountains they are more accustomed to a winter situation where they are buried in snow. In that situation they are actually moisture-deprived, as the moisture in the snow is unavailable to the plant. For many of us in more temperate climates, winter is not a time of snow but of winter wet. Therefore, at a time when the semp plant is accustomed to being moisture-deprived it now receives substantial moisture.

Some of the plants do show adaptations to this, with the cobwebbed types losing their cobwebs. Generally the satin cultivars are fine even with the winter wet, but cultivars with very pubescent leaves or with heavy cilia can show damage, often rotting. A combination of extra moist conditions and a strong and sudden cold spell can be especially devastating to these cultivars. For example, 'Shirley's Joy' was never injured in the cold winters of Massachusetts, but in rainy Oregon, the leaves are often damaged by the rain and sudden cold. If your collection is in pots, move the pots into a cold frame, not so much as to protect them from cold, but to limit the moisture the plants receive. Greg Colucci, in winter rain heavy Seattle, Washington, grows his plants in troughs and covers the entire trough with plastic to stop any rain from hitting the plants. In a garden situation this is more difficult, but if only a few scattered cultivars are affected a pane of glass or a clear plastic covering can be placed over the most sensitive species. For those of us not wanting to go to these extremes, planting only winter wet-resistant cultivars such as the many satin ones may be the best alternative. I have also potted a few special cultivars and just put them on my protected patio, rather than grow them in the open.

Fig. 6-3. In a wet winter situation cobweb and velvet cultivars can be damaged or killed.

Summer Heat and Humidity

Most people consider semps to be full sun plants. In favorable areas, such as the British Isles, northern continental Europe, and parts of the Pacific Northwest, this can mostly be true. However, even in these favorable areas sudden extremes of temperature and/or excessively high humidity can profoundly affect the plants, setting up rot conditions, loss of many of the leaves, and loss of the offsets. When such weather is predicted in otherwise more benign climates, covering the beds with shade cloth will alleviate the stress. Summer 2016 was especially miserable in Oregon, with a record number of days approaching 100°F.

Shade cloth covering during these days eliminated damage to the plants. Plants not covered or growing in some shade did not fare as well. In areas where conditions in summer are normally hot and humid growing the plants in some shade is definitely an advantage. My friend, Reiner Kloth, grew a fine crop of semps in his garden in Mississippi, but with a fifty percent shade cloth.

DISEASES

Semps do suffer from the rust fungus *Endophylllum sempervivi*, which will cause a lopsided growth of the rosette. I have never seen this fungus in any plant in my garden, although I have destroyed a few plants that looked suspect, when one side of a rosette was much more elongated than the other side for no apparent reason. These did not go into the compost, but rather were wrapped in plastic and put in the garbage. Apparently, it is a slowly spreading fungus and rarely do other plants even in the clump show damage.

Especially during really wet conditions, one often finds a single rosette or two that will for some reason have all the leaves turn brown and go mushy, eventually rotting entirely. Occasionally one sees signs of the black spores typical of *Botrytis* or webbed fungi, but I almost doubt that these are the initial causative agent; rather, something that occurs as a consequence of the damage that has occurred to the rosette. I do routinely pull out these rosettes and destroy them. I have never attempted to save them, as generally they are a minor portion of a clump. When seedlings do this they are discarded, as I do not want weak plants to be put on the market and distributed. Some of our commercial growers use a fungicidal treatment such as Subdue® as a preventative measure, but I think for us gardeners growing the plants with good culture will solve much of these problems, except in extreme conditions of rain and/or humidity and temperature.

CHAPTER 7

HYBRIDIZING SEMPERVIVUM

INTRODUCTION

Hybridizing may seem daunting to those who have not tried it, but it really involves just a couple technical steps: emasculating the flowers, protecting the flowers from insect pollination, and transferring pollen to the stigma. None of these are very difficult. Pat Drown and I did this as nine-year-olds and made hybrids that were introduced to the market, so being a rocket scientist is *not* required to make this all happen. Learning a few of the tricks will help you do much better than with random crossings. Pat and I had Polly Bishop to explain all of this to us. Polly had gathered all the necessary equipment to do this, but the equipment is easy to obtain and inexpensive for anyone wishing to make an attempt.

In this chapter I describe the methods for raising seedlings from open pollinated seed, plus all of the techniques associated with crossing semps. As you start doing this, you will probably find that modifications of this method work best for you based on your climate and gardening situation.

THE SKROCKI METHOD

For those who prefer a more lazy way of producing hybrids, simply grow seed from stalks in your garden that bees or other insects have pollinated. Ed Skrocki was the most vocal proponent of this method, and it has been dubbed the "Skrocki method" by all those who use it. Gary Gossett further refined the method by only allowing the bloomstalks of the most colorful and choice cultivars to come into bloom so that bees could only make crosses between these cultivars. He also grouped the *heuffelii* cultivars together so that they would cross with each other, rather than being self-pollinated if they were grown in a more isolated situation. Certainly the high quality of Gary's Pacific series speaks volumes for this technique. Even Ed eventually decided not to harvest all of his seed and began selectively harvesting from parents that he figured had the highest chances of producing worthwhile progeny. Toward the end of his career he even concentrated on just the cobwebbed and tufted sorts. Polly Bishop added yet another way of improving the odds. She argued that we know so little of the genetics of dark foliage color that the best approach would be to do intercrosses between all of the darkest ones. Instead of doing this by hand, Polly transplanted the blooming rosettes of all the darkest semps in her garden to a common spot, then crisscrossed the stalks, so the bees would go from one parent to another regularly. She then gathered all of that seed and planted it out. From several hundred seedlings she selected 'Plumb Rose' and 'Dark Cloud,' which were some of the darkest then available. 'Dark Cloud' has since proven to be a powerful parent in its own right.

Although I do not use open pollinated seed as a matter of course, I have obtained seeds from cultivars I do not own but want to use in my breeding program. The other cultivars I leave to be pollinated by bees are ones that are not too fertile. Bees may find compatible mates for these cultivars, whereas I might waste weeks of time crossing only to have no seed. For example, cultivars from the tufted types are often of limited fertility, so bees might be more successful than I am in obtaining any seeds. When I was first involved in crossing semps, I would often test the potential of a given parent. For example, I grew open-pollinated seed from 'Missouri Rose,' 'Purdy's 70-40,' and other of the best cultivars of the day to determine if it was worth using that parent further in crossing. From these I also selected seedlings that were superior to their parent in some characteristics, and these were used in further crosses.

So why would you want to waste time crossing if successful breeders such as Ed Skrocki, Polly Bishop, and Gary Gossett all used open pollinated seeds? For one, you dramatically increase your odds of creating the hybrid you want to produce, instead of allowing a random mating by chance to produce what you want. I described this phenomenon to Ed in terms of dog breeding. At the time, Bill Nixon was raising dachshunds and Pat Drown-Warner's dad was breeding Siberian huskies. Even though both strains of dogs produced beautiful puppies, one can only imagine the awful combination of traits if these two lines were combined. Mutts only a mother could love! The bees are making these same kind of indiscriminate crosses and creating the plant equivalent of these mutts. Of course, bees occasionally make just the right cross, too. It is fun to grow new plants from seed, and you may beat all the odds and get a pretty one. I want to guide and advance my lines toward specific goals. Only planned crosses will get you to these goals without throwing away many seedlings. Moreover, I find the overall quality of my seedlings is very high and I do not mind giving away any of the seedlings, because they are better than ninety-nine percent of the cultivars on the market. Essentially, I have eliminated those semp versions of the "dachshund X husky" crosses.

PLANNING YOUR CROSSES

It is more difficult to make hand crosses than simply growing plants from seed, but hand crosses allow you to combine specific parents that might get you closer to your goals than the random crossing caused by bees. For example, Ed Skrocki grew nearly 20,000 seedlings each year from open-pollinated seed, but as a teenager in Massachusetts I grew but several hundred, mostly from planned crosses, and also named many seedlings. Ed is right, in that plant breeding is a game of numbers: the more one grows, the greater the chance of selecting something good. Right now I grow about 6,000 seedlings from my hand crosses each year, and this will give me six to ten cultivars that I will introduce to the market. Another fifty or so seedlings are saved for further breeding.

First, it is wise to establish some goals for your breeding project. Random crosses between cultivars are not much better than what bees do! For example, one of my goals is to make semps the size of footballs and black. That is a *long* range goal, but it does guide me in my crosses. So in a given season, I deliberately cross all the largest and darkest semps with each other. Actually, my inspiration for this project comes from looking at some of the very dark *Echevaria* cultivars that combine these characteristics and are especially striking, but of course not hardy in most climates. What we see in related succulent plants, such as *Aeonium* or *Echevaria*, is probably also obtainable in semps. With each seedling crop I get closer to my goal of huge black rosettes, and these seedlings become the parents of the next generation. A simpler goal might be "improving cultivar X." For example, you admire the spring coloration of a particular cultivar, but the color does not last for a full season. Crossing this cultivar with one that has excellent color retention might give you just what you wanted, as well as some surprises that have colorations between the two parents. When I am planning crosses, I try to envision in my head what the combination of the two parents might be. In my garden 'Jungle Shadows' grows next to 'Lilac Time.' Several years ago both were blooming, and although initially I had no intent to make the cross, the more I thought about something with the form of 'Lilac Time' and the colors of 'Jungle Shadows,' the more I liked it and the cross was consummated. This turned out to be one of the happiest combinations of my hybridizing career, with several plants with unique colors that are slated for market. These included good quality pinks, odd greyed pinks, and some huge dark rosettes with water lily form. As these seedlings bloomed they were both self- and sib-crossed to see all the possible combinations of the characteristics from these very diverse parents. As I look at these seedlings in the patch right now, I can see every combination of the traits of these two parents. An extremely wide and amazing near black is very exciting, as are some beautiful pinks with much more intense pink coloring than 'Lilac Time.' A couple of these are being evaluated for possible naming, as they combine characteristics not present together in other existing cultivars.

People are often surprised that I do a lot of self-pollinations of my plants. Most semps have either unknown parents, or only the pod (female) parent is known. By self-pollinating that plant I can learn a bit about the parents of that plant, and also have a good idea as to the fertility of the plant. Tufted semps are always hybrids between a cobwebbed type and a non-cobweb, or an advanced generation of such a cross. By self-pollinating tufted plants, you begin to see the characteristics of both the cobweb and non-cobweb parents segregate out, and recessive characters not seen in the parent plant become exposed. For example, here is a description of a group of seedlings from Ed Skrocki's cultivar 'Fluffy Fluke' X self. In these seedling rows there are many degrees of cobwebbing, from just small tufts of hairs at the leaf tip to nearly full cobwebs. Size varies from quite small up through about medium-sized leaves. Color also varies tremendously from plain green through orange and reds, plus some that are strong bicolors. Although 'Fluffy Fluke' is itself an interesting plant, the combination of recessive characters and dominant ones that may be expressed in individual seedlings allows for the potential of this plant to be more fully explored. Many of these tufted types have reduced fertility, so it is wise to repeat this cross many times to obtain enough seedlings. Some of the roller types are difficult to self-pollinate, probably because of the plants having mechanisms to prevent/discourage such pollinations. For example, I only obtained eight seedlings from self-pollinating an entire bloomstalk of flowers on 'S. Emerald Spring.'

A lot of my current breeding lines start with the cultivar 'Killer.' This cultivar intrigued me right away, as it had many phases of color, although all of them were colorful and some are very intense. Looking at its known pod parent, it bore little resemblance to that plant in shape or color, so I knew that it was a fairly different pollen parent that was the father to 'Killer.' Not surprisingly, the ('Killer' X self) cross gave a large variety of colors and sizes from the small shiny red 'Red Hot Chili' to the much larger and variable rose-pink 'Gwen's Rose,' and watermarked large red 'Fashion Diva,' as well as a number of red and green bicolors with different levels of saturation and extent of color. Leaf shapes varied from short and narrow to broad and long, and everything in between. What excitement it was to grow this seedling crop! These seedlings were then crossed with each other and also with a group of similarly interesting seedlings from 'Jungle Shadows' X self.

As the bloom season begins, I make a list of all the cultivars that are blooming and I begin to plan what sort of crosses to make. I write all these potential combinations down in a notebook, and as the flowers start to progress I make final decisions as to what crosses I will make; that way I have a plan before anything starts to bloom. Not all semps bloom at the same time. The cobwebs are generally the first to bloom, so you may only be able to use the last blossoms on these cultivars with the first blooms on others. This bloom season difference may alter some of your plans in crossing. In the latter sections of this chapter I will discuss some of the genetic considerations I use in making decisions for cultivars to cross.

MAKING THE CROSS

The *Sempervivum* flower lends itself to cross-pollination, as the pollen-bearing anthers mature before the stigma of that flower is receptive to pollen. Before any flower opens, I take a paper bag and place it over the developing stalk. I can use paper in Oregon because we rarely see rain in the summer. If you live in a wetter summer climate, you might want to use muslin bags, or even cast off pieces of panty hose to cover the stalk. Muslin or panty hose have the advantage of letting in more light and air than paper bags. My first year in Oregon, I added a rubber band to the bottom of the paper bag to help secure it to the stalk, although pollinating insects seem not to crawl in, even though the bag is open at the bottom. On the larger stalks, the bag tends to stay in place because the branches on the stalk are tightly appressed to the edge of the bag. On smaller stalks, a rubber band around the bottom of the paper bag is a more useful addition, as the bags tend to blow away, especially on the small and tightly branched stalks of the cobweb varieties. I have also used the stakes used for markers of daylilies and other taller perennials in my garden to support the bag and ensure it will stay in place. Position the marker in the soil next to the bloomstalk and slip the bag over the stalk and the stake. This seems to be especially helpful on the short and thin stalks of the cobweb types which are less rigid too. If you use paper bags, write the cross you intend to make on the bag. I re-read this label each morning before making the cross so I do not make a mistake and use the wrong pollen parent. Besides this record, I also keep a log book of my crosses and mark the branch that has been pollinated with fine colored wire as a further memory aid if I do not pollinate the entire stalk. The convention of plant breeders in recording crosses is to list the pod or female parent first, followed by an X and then the pollen or paternal parent. For example, a cross using 'Killer' as the pod parent and 'Jungle Shadows' as the pollen parent would be recorded as 'Killer' X 'Jungle Shadows.'

Fig. 7-1. A flower with petals just unfurling and pollen sacks not yet dehisced. At this stage, the pollen sacks should be removed from the pod parent.

Fig. 7-2. A branch of a flowering stock with a flower at the same stage as in Fig. 7-1, one at a perfect stage to use as a pollen parent, and one ready to be pollinated.

Now that your stalk is protected from insects, you will have a job each day for several weeks. The first thing you must do is remove the swollen anthers from the developing flowers that are going to be your pod or female parent. I find that Dumont #5 tweezers are ideal for this purpose; they have a very sharp and narrow tip that can grab and remove the little ball-like anthers with ease. If you are like me, you will want to have several pairs of these tweezers, as I tend to lose them somewhere in the garden. If you intend to self-pollinate a cultivar, do not emasculate the flower. Rather, simply keep the plant covered and use the anthers that have dehisced to pollinate stigmas that are receptive. Now you have a several-day wait until the stigma of the emasculated flower becomes receptive. I often describe the stage when the stigmas become receptive as a "crown rack of lamb," as the flower spreads the stigmas out toward the edge of the petals. They should feel slightly sticky to the touch. At this point, I grab a flower with lovely ripe pollen that I have protected in another bag, but one in which

I have not removed the anthers. The pollen should be a lovely bright yellow and fluffy. You can do the pollination by simply rubbing the pollen-laden flower over the top of the pod parent, or you can remove anthers, take the tweezers, and rub them over the tops of the stigma. What works best for me is to use the Dumont #5 tweezers' sharp tips to snip off the pollen-laden flower from the stalk. I then stick the tongs of the tweezers into the base of the flower, so I have the flower secured at the end of the forceps. I then use the flower to paint pollen on a number of flowers. Other people use a fine camel's hair brush for this pollen transfer. Take the brush and drag it over the yellow anthers until you see pollen on the brush, then run the brush across the stop of the stigmas. With a magnifying glass you should be able to see that the tips of the stigmas are now coated with pollen. Mary Mitchell (1976) describes her method as "shaking pollen" from the pollen parent over the flower of the pod parent. I do not have good luck shaking the pollen off and getting the pollen where I want it! You may have better luck than I did with this technique. I perform this crossing routine as part of my regular garden routine. In Massachusetts, the pollen seemed to develop a bit more quickly than it does in Oregon, so most of my crosses here take place between nine and ten o'clock in the morning. Later in the day also seems to work, and I generally give the same flower pollen for several days to maximize my chances of success pollinating that flower. If you use brushes, be sure to clean them between different pollen parents, or else the contaminating pollen may be the one that is involved in the fertilization. A simple dip of the brush tip in rubbing alcohol will kill all the pollen on the brush. Let the brush dry thoroughly (I use a paper towel to ensure it is dry) before collecting more pollen. I pollinate all of the flowers on a branch, or even multiple branches, as I seem not to be as efficient as bees in getting seed. By performing the cross on ten to twenty flowers you will have enough seed to learn something about the potential of these parents.

The flowers of the rollers and *heuffelii* types are campanulate flowers that are more difficult to emasculate, because the petals so tightly enclose the anthers. For these flowers, I use very fine-tipped clippers and remove all the petals and anthers from the flower to be used as a pod parent. For the pollen parent, I cut the petals off and use the whole flower, with its fluffy yellow pollen, to cross on to the pod parent. Otherwise the technique is identical to the other semps. The rollers bloom very infrequently in Oregon, so I tend not to make many crosses with them. They have never been my favorites, as they seem to be a lot less variable than the semps in colors, sizes, and shapes. I think there is also much room for improvement, as many of the best cultivars are merely collected clones. There may be some self-incompatibility in the roller types too, as I got very little seed from self-pollinating 'Emerald Spring,' but a good bit when I crossed it with *S. soboliferum ssp. allionii* 'Yellow Green Form.' Gary Gossett reported that open-pollinated seed of the rarely blooming *ssp. arenaria*

Fig. 7-3. A flower with stamens in a "rack of lamb" configuration.

Fig. 7-4. Flower stalk with seeds at various stages of maturation.

gave seedlings that were almost all from pollination of *heuffelii*, rather than its own pollen. These data indicate that an effective way of producing roller X *heuffelii* types would be to place plants of blooming *heuffelii* cultivars adjacent to blooming rollers.

In climates not as amenable to crossing as Oregon, it is useful to actually dig and pot the blooming plants and put them in an isolated, dry area, such as a covered deck or patio, and then cage them all with netting to prevent insect contamination. This also makes it easier to make crosses between plants that might be separated by long distances in your garden. Moving the plants does not seem to affect the ability of these plants to set seed.

Two to three days after the last flower on a branch has been pollinated, you can remove the paper bag or other covering and allow the seed to continue to develop. At this point the stigmas are no longer receptive and bees can do no further pollination to interfere with the cross. Watch these stalks carefully, as you do not want to lose the seed after doing all this careful work.

SEED HARVEST

For the Skrocki method, you harvest all of the seeds on the stalk. The seed on the bloomstalk matures from the basal flowers, nearest the main stalk, to the ends of each blooming branch. As a consequence, if you wait until the last flowers on the seed stalk mature, the earliest flowers might have already dispersed their seed. To maximize the number of seeds collected, I let the seed stalk mature so that the basal flower's seed capsules are on the verge of opening (the top of the follicles will open at their tips) and the terminal seed capsules are just matured (gone brownish), but are not at all open. On a very still day (just after the dew has gone from the grass in the morning is a good time), go into the garden and very carefully clip the base of the stalk and invert it into a smaller paper bag, such as those used for lunches. Keep the bloomstalk upright until you are right over the bag so the seed is not spilled from the capsules. Label the bag with the name of the cultivar and bring the stalk into a shaded, dry place, such as a garage or garden shed, for the seed capsules to ripen and dry. When the seed stalk is completely dry (generally in September or October in Oregon), I give the bag a gentle patting between my hands to release the seed from the follicles and then invert the bag while holding the bloomstalk in the bag over a large piece of white paper that has been folded in the middle and then flattened. Most of the seed, as well as some of the chaff and some small leaves, will fall out, but what falls to the paper will be many of the seeds. I then fold the paper back up, pushing the seed toward the fold, and discard the more obvious pieces of chaff. Decant the seed gently into glassine envelopes (ones used by stamp collectors with no glue on the envelope lip) and then fold the envelope so that the seed is sealed away from the open edges of the envelope. Place the folded glassine envelope in a coin envelope to prevent any loss of the tiny seeds from the envelope. Label the envelope with the seed parent X pollen parent and seal the coin envelope. I denote bee pollinated seed as "OP" for "open pollinated." To keep the seed fresh, store the collection of seed envelopes in a sealed plastic bag or glass jar in the crisper area of the refrigerator until you are ready to plant. Mark Smith (1979) showed that semp seeds require this cold vernalization to germinate most successfully. Erwin Geiger (personal communication) stores his seed in the freezer portion of the refrigerator; because semp seeds are quite dry, this procedure does not affect germination as it does for other seed with higher moisture content. Seeds from Erwin that have been stored in the freezer and then shipped to the US have germinated well.

Ed Skrocki (2003) used several modifications of these techniques. Carefully harvesting on a windless day, Ed cut the stalks that were nearly dry and placed the stalks in a two inch deep baking pan (he also used a shoe box early in his career). He mixed all the different seed stalks together, rather than separating out each stalk for the particular pod parent. Once inside, he cut all but the seed-bearing areas of the stalk off. By not cutting these areas off outdoors he reduced the chances of spilling seed from the seed capsules, as too much shaking is likely to dislodge the seed. The stalks are shaken over the pan and allowed to collect along the bottom of the pan. The remaining pieces of stalk are placed over paper and allowed to drop more seed. Ed used two filters to separate the chaff from the seed.

Because semp seed is so tiny, chaff can interfere with germination, although I have not found this to be much of a problem except in seed lots where there are very few seeds and lots of chaff. Some tufted forms that have low fertility are often the worst in this respect, and Ed was using these cultivars heavily toward the end of his hybridizing career. Ed also sold seed to Park's and Thompson and Morgan's seed companies, and they required that the seed be clear of any chaff.

For the seed raised from hand crosses, I gather the seed and place it in paper bags to dry similarly to the open pollinated methods described. Because I want to see *every* seed from these crosses, often times I merely crumble the seed capsules into the glassine envelopes, ensuring that every seed is saved. I also make sure that any seed from the bag is also placed in the glassine envelope. Bees are much more effective pollinators, so the number of seed/flower tends to be less when you perform the cross. That is one reason I try to pollinate at least ten, and preferably more than twenty flowers for any given cross so that at least thirty or so seedlings will result.

PLANTING SEED

For planting, I use eight inch pots filled to within several inches of the top with a commercial potting mix that is fresh from the bag and allowed to wet thoroughly overnight or longer. It should be thoroughly wet, but not dripping. Moss, liverworts, and other small winter weeds such as bittercress are ubiquitous here in the Pacific Northwest, so if you can get the seedlings up and growing before these plant pests invade the pot, the better off your seedlings will be. Generally, I open the bag of prepared potting mix just before filling the pots so that the soil has minimal chance of being exposed to the spores or seeds of these pest plants. Before planting the seeds, I gently flatten the surface of the potting mix with the palm of my hand. Using the flap of the glassine envelope as a way to regulate seed distribution, I gently sprinkle the seed over the surface of the pot to spread the seed as evenly as possible over the surface of the potting mix. Semp seeds are tiny, and it is very easy to plant them too thickly. Some growers even put the seed in a pepper shaker and use it to spread the seed more thinly and evenly across the potting mixture. When in doubt, use multiple pots rather than trying to get all the seed into a single pot. Some growers use flats rather than pots because the surface area of the flat is greater and it is a bit easier to spread the seed more evenly across the surface. I prefer pots because I can more easily carry them to my beds for rowing out the seedlings. Generally, I plan this planting of new seed right before a gentle rain is due and when wind is at an absolute minimum. Planting semp seed in a strong wind is a waste of time, unless your goal is to spread semps throughout your county! If wind is an issue, do all the planting in an enclosed area, such as a garage or porch. If no rain is in sight, a gentle sprinkling of the seed pots is a good idea to settle the seed into the potting compost. In some instances, I have covered the seed with a very fine layer of sand. The sand might inhibit moss spore germination to some extent, but otherwise seems to not be of much benefit for seed germination. Regardless of how you plant, put a good quality label in the pot. I use aluminum labels marked with a soft lead pencil. The pencil marking persists well at least through three to four seasons. This label goes with the seedlings to the row out beds. I keep a bound notebook that records a number for each seed lot, and that number is also recorded on the label. This numbering system will be discussed later in this chapter, but I also use this labeling system for the open pollinated seed that I plant.

When to plant is a matter of your climate. In Oregon, I start my seed in February or early March. This is around a month before the worst killing frosts are over. My pots are placed in a sheltered location that receives little chance of frost but is exposed to the elements. The pots should be kept moist, so if you live in a climate where late winter or early spring rains are not usual, vigilance on keeping the pots moist is a must, and even more so as the seed begins to germinate. The roots of the seedlings are tiny, and a few days of dry potting mix can mean death for them. Generally, within ten to fourteen days of planting and with reasonable temperatures,

Fig. 7-5. Pot with young seedlings ready for transplanting.

you will begin to see small green specks in the seed pots. These first two leaves are actually cotyledons that have lipids and proteins that will be used to help the young seedling develop roots and true leaves. The potting mix I use has some fertilizer in it to help sustain growth of the seedlings. A weak fertilizer such as those used in transplanting seedlings is also given to the young seedlings every two weeks until they are rowed out.

When a frost or freeze is predicted either cover the seed pots with Reemay or other frost-preventing fabric, or move the seedling pots to a protected location, such as a garage or porch. Lynn Smith fashions protected pots using gallon plastic jugs with a portion of the side cut open and the pot filled halfway with soil mix. This system protects the seedlings from the rigors of the outside world much better than a simple pot, but it may be more difficult to extract the seedlings from the pot, especially if they come up densely.

If you do not wish to do all this work but still want to plant some seed, there are some easier protocols that work remarkably well. When I was a kid in Massachusetts, I did not plant my seed in pots, but rather cleared an area of an existing bed and scattered the seed along the row, with a marker at the end of the row. Another approach is to plant in an area of the yard not likely to be disturbed. I had several big clumps of deciduous daylilies at my folks' property and would scatter seed in back of these clumps, put a marker for the seed that was planted, and let them be until germination started in the spring. In those days, I planted the seed in the fall, partly because I was away at school and planting in the soil did not require any extensive care on my part. I am sure that I had lower numbers of seedlings than I might have, had I used more optimum conditions, but I still rowed out a good number of seedlings each spring. An even lazier approach is to simply put dried stalks in areas of the garden that are relatively undisturbed. The seeds will fall from the stalks and seedlings will appear in this area. This method will produce mostly gobs of seedlings that are very close together and difficult to separate.

I have never raised much seed indoors, although I did start some seed on a windowsill at my folks' home when I was a kid. The plants grew all winter long, but many were etiolated by the time I rowed out the seedlings in the spring. George Mendl has the most elaborate indoor growth conditions I have ever seen. He has rather high intensity grow lights placed directly above the plants. After seeing these photos, I felt very low-tech about my own seed raising techniques.

Fig. 7-6 and 7-7. Elaborate controlled conditions for seedling growth.

ROWING OUT SEEDLINGS

Opinions differ greatly as to when seedlings should be rowed out. I generally transplant after the majority of seedlings in the pot have four true leaves (that is six total, including the cotyledons) and before the seed pots are too crowded. The seedlings are still tiny at this point, and it is a bit difficult working with such small plants. If the seedlings are transferred early to the seedling bed, the plants seem to mature more rapidly, and generally, in four to six months, the plants start to make increase. If you feel too nervous about rowing out the plants at this stage, you have two other good options:

1)   leave the plants in the pot to grow for a season and transplant the much larger seedlings, then;

2)   transfer the seedlings to pots or flats and continue to grow them under these more controlled situations.

I use raised beds to grow my seedlings—much as I use for named cultivars—that have roughly eight inches of soil in them. The seedlings are well raised above the level of the garden paths, ensuring good drainage. The beds I use are approximately six feet across, but I have very long arms. (You should design a bed so that you can easily reach to the center of the bed to plant the seedlings.) The beds are filled with a sterile growing mix from a local nursery that I buy by the truckload that is described as "premium perennial mix." It has good water retaining ability, but is lighter than most topsoils. Because tiny seedlings are very sensitive to weed pressure, the final inch of soil in the bed is removed and replaced by a very clean potting soil similar or identical in composition to that used for the pots used to germinate the seed. Wet the soil down thoroughly before attempting to plant the seedlings.

Extracting the seedlings from the pots is a bit of a trick. The potting mix that I use forms a bit of a crust, and I use a small salad fork or a prong from my hand fork to lift up small pieces of crusted potting soil with the tiny seedlings still attached. This procedure helps maintain soil contact with the tiny roots of the seedlings. Generally, the pieces of crusted potting soil and the attached seedlings can be gently pressed into the soil mix in the seedling bed. Within the pot, I work from the less crowded areas toward the more densely covered areas. Soil from the bottom of the pot not containing seed is distributed over the bed.

Plant the seedlings in straight rows, with about one to two inches between the seedlings and about four to six inches between the rows to allow for growth of the seedlings through at least one year. I use a transplanting fertilizer on the seedlings at the time of transplanting. The area between the seedlings is mulched with a very fine layer of grit to suppress weed growth, prevent soil splash-up, and maintain moist conditions. These seedlings will need careful attention. They should never want for moisture, nor should they be sopping wet, either. Daily inspection is required. The markers from the pots are used to mark the beginning of the seed group or cross.

When rowing out the seedlings, I try to put contrasting colors or types of seedlings next to each other, so it is very clear when one cross begins and ends. For example, a cross for cobwebbed types might be adjacent to a cross of roller types. Birds and other animals (or visitors wanting to look at the cross records!) will sometimes move the labels. I also chart the seedling bed as I am rowing out the seedlings so that I know how many rows of seedlings of a particular group I have. These charts are invaluable in establishing any doubtful markings of a particular seedling group.

It seems as soon as you plant out the seedlings every creature on Earth tries to disrupt the planting! Birds are probably the most destructive. I cover the entire seedling bed with bird mesh. This does not make the bed particularly beautiful, but it does protect your seedlings from being unearthed. The Steller jays in the Pacific Northwest are particularly curious and will go after labels, as well as the small plants. Cats can be another problem. These raised beds full of nice, fluffy soil look suspiciously like a very nice cat box to all the cats in the neighborhood. If cats are present in your neighborhood, the bird netting will dissuade cats as well. By the end of the season, the seedlings will have grown into a solid mass of plants and are much less affected by any sort of animal, save deer or elk.

After the seedlings are rowed out, this is no time to be resting on the back porch! The seedlings should never want for water, nor have weeds growing around them that might

Fig. 7-8. Bird netting over a seedling bed to protect the young seedlings.

inhibit growth. I use a transplanting fertilizer such as Quick Start® on the seedlings every other week. This forces the seedlings into very good growth, and by the end of the summer a majority of the plants will start producing offsets. The fertilizing regime should be slowed as fall approaches so the plants have a chance to harden off before colder weather approaches. Because I am selecting for plants that perform under real weather conditions, I do not cover or coddle the plants through our wet and cold winters by covering them with plastic. I want other gardeners not to be shocked by poor growth of a seedling I have brought to the market.

MARKING THE SELECTED SEEDLINGS

Now that you have found some interesting seedlings in your plantings, you want to be able to identify them so that you can record your evaluations of these plants. When I collect the seeds from my crosses, I give each cross a number in my notebook. I use a simple system where a letter denotes the year of collection. For example, the "E" series are from seed collected in 2014. Each cross is then given a number, so for example, a cross of 'Gwen's Rose' X 'Fashion Diva' is given the notation E45. This number goes on the pot label and is transferred to the row outs; it is also recorded in a hardbound notebook. When I start to select seedlings to retain, I label the seedling with the number of the cross and then a dash with the seedling number, so the second seedling selected from the 'Gwen's Rose' X 'Fashion Diva' is E45-2. This allows me to immediately recognize siblings from a cross by their seedling number. Other people use much simpler labeling methods. Ed Skrocki simply marked his sequentially by number, so seedling #51 was the fifty-first seedling he selected.

Now the selected ones should be transferred to a bed where they are grown on and evaluated over several seasons. This will allow the seedling to go through a number of different weather regimes. I find it helpful to use the criteria listed (see the following section) in evaluating the seedlings, as it forces me to consider all the aspects of the plant. I can't just be dazzled by the spring color and forget that the plant is not a good grower, or is frequently damaged by winter wet or cold.

Fig. 7-9. Bed of selected seedlings being trialed.

EVALUATING THE SEEDLINGS

When you first see the bewildering array of colors and patterns in the seedlings, your first impulse might be to keep them all. Sanity then generally returns, and you realize that although there are some good ones, there are many that are too similar to their parents. To aid in evaluating your seedlings, here are the criteria I use to evaluate mine. We have used these criteria in evaluating seedlings and named cultivars in the Hybridizing Clinics that have occurred in my yard for the last several years. Each of the participants learned to pick out the better cultivars and to look at all aspects of a plant.

Many of our most productive hybridizers have never made a real cross, but what they have been is excellent *selectors* of plants. That is, they can recognize a quality plant, choose an interesting name for it, and market it successfully. Many of these breeders know the criteria by which cultivars are selected innately, but for others, learning these criteria helps us evaluate which plants are the best from our crosses. We may even learn that we have made a bad batch of seedlings and we need to increase the size of our compost pile!

— THE ROSETTE —

This is the most important characteristic in judging *Sempervivum* seedlings; the flowers can only either augment or detract from the value of a cultivar minimally. Within the rosette evaluation, there are certain categories that are evaluated.

Overall Form

Does the rosette lie flat to the ground, or does it produce more of an upright look? The very open waterlily-type forms are very appealing, especially in a larger rosette. In general, very symmetrical forms are most pleasing to the eye, so whatever form the rosette takes, symmetry is considered a virtue. Plants that produce leaves that grow more on one side than the other, or produce leaves of different sizes or shapes that distort the symmetry, are considered a fault. Exceptions to this are forms that are purposefully not symmetrical, such as 'Fuzzy Wuzzy,' that produces numerous crested rosettes or double forms, and totally wild forms like 'Weirdo.' These forms are more conversation pieces than beautiful, and should be a minority in any collection. Some of these might be pretty, others not. Symmetry is best when a rosette is grown in isolation so that the plant is not crowded by neighboring rosettes. Cultivars that keep their symmetry, even in a crowded clump, are especially favored. Helen Payne was an extreme advocate for symmetry in semp cultivars. She thought it was most perfect not only when the rosette was symmetrical, but when the offsets were also arranged symmetrically around the mother rosette. She described this as the "wreath form." When she introduced my 'Silvertone,' she was so excited that *every* rosette would make these perfect wreaths and illustrated that in her book.

Number, Shape, and Width of Leaves

There is almost an infinite variety of leaf lengths, widths, and shapes that add to the distinction of a given cultivar. The tips of the leaves can go to very sharp points or widen at the tip, so that the tip area has a softer look. Much as for the overall rosette form, the symmetry of the plant will be improved if the leaves are of similar dimensions and shape across the plant. A fault would be producing leaves that are very irregular in any of these characteristics. Leaf characteristics that add distinction are leaves of exceptional width—either very wide or very narrow—unusual forms, such as the tubular forms in 'Oddity,' or increased width of leaves as in 'Plastic.'

Size

Rosettes range in size from ⅛ in. to over twelve inches in diameter. There is no preferred size of a rosette, but sizes that are novel for their type are considered most positively.

Thus, a large cobwebbed type, which are normally small, would be considered a positive. Conversely, a glabrous small red might be more distinctive than a medium-sized one. Generally larger rosettes are showier, but have the disadvantage that when they bloom, they leave bigger gaps in the clumps. As a hybridizer, we should know our prejudices in judging sizes if we prefer one size over another and judge the plant on its merits. I am talking to myself here, as I generally pick out the larger seedlings when some of the smaller ones are really better plants.

Color

In general, bright and clear colors are considered most desirable. In the days when I started breeding, there were few cultivars with good strong coloration, whereas now strong reds and purples are more common. Blended colors can be very attractive if the overall effect is not dull. When I first started breeding semps, many of the cultivars were drab shades of olive overlaid with a bit of red-purple anthocyanin. It made for a very dirty effect. Unique colors, such as the beetroot color of 'Borscht,' or near black cultivars such as 'Patent Leather Shoes,' are looked upon favorably. Cultivars that retain their color during the year or change colors to pleasing shades are considered the best in these categories. Although in the past cultivars that faded rapidly were more common, this would be considered a fault in newly named cultivars. Colors that have unusual winter color are also favored. Some, such as 'Michael,' have a new color in the winter, and these stand out in a planting. Watermarks often add distinction to the basic color of the rosette. Although patterns in green and red have become common, bicolors in unusual shades of green and purple, rather than red, would be unique and welcome. Some colors in the *Sempervivum* are still lacking, such as good clear pinks, near blacks, and clean lavenders. Improvements in these colors would be

Fig. 7-10. Watermarks created by bands of wax that affect the coloring of the leaf.

especially welcome. We are still far from black, orange, and pink. Progress in these colors would definitely be something to save in a seedling, even though it might not have other good qualities. Brown or bronze cultivars are fairly rare, and improvements in brightness or depth in these colors, or in larger sizes, would be good additions. Not many silver-leaved plants have been introduced lately, even though these are especially useful in contrasting with darker shades. Development of bluer *Sempervivum* has seemingly stagnated. Blue color often develops best later in the season, so extending blue color throughout the season would be an asset. Greens are still needed, especially those with chartreuse and olive-toned ones, or those with highly contrasted tip colors. Gold colors or variegated leaves are especially welcome, even more so if the rosette has good vigor.

Texture

The texture of the leaf is determined by the presence of small or large hairs, plus a number of surface waxes. Shiny leaves have abundant wax that is applied smoothly to the leaf surface. Shiny surfaces often make the color seem brighter. Satin leaves have wax, but it is present in a less smooth layer, often in the form of wax crystals. These satin leaves soften the color underneath and often mimic a look of being lightly powdered. Most of the blues and silver rosettes are actually an illusion of these colors created by the satin overlying the basic color of the rosette. Velvety leaves have tiny epidermal hairs distributed densely across the surface of the leaf, whereas cilia are longer hairs clustered at the leaf edges. The velvety texture tends to make the colors look darker, or occasionally dull. Cilia add brightness to the leaf, adding almost a white edge, like frosting on a cake. In full cobwebs, the hairs at the tips of the leaves are dense and long, forming a complete covering. These hairs are made of pectin, and help the cobweb absorb water from dew, as well as protect the rosette. Hybrids of cobwebs and non-cobwebs have tufts of hair on each leaf, but the hairs are shorter and not connected. There is no preferred texture, but it can influence the overall beauty of the plant and add to its distinctiveness.

Health

Does the plant go through the winter with a minimum of dead leaves? Does the plant take the high humidity and heat in summer? Does the plant produce sufficient increase? If the answer to any of these questions is *no* then you need to evaluate whether the pampering is worth it. No one wants to grow a problem grower when there are so many easy growers. One's interpretations should be tempered a bit by the growing conditions, such as extremes of cold and moisture. If winter or summer conditions are so brutal that most cultivars look damaged, then some leniency in evaluation should take place. Comparing the plant's health with other cultivars of similar colors and sizes will allow for a more realistic interpretation of the seedling's health. For example, velvety leaves are much more prone to problems with winter wet. Seedlings with velvet leaves that are less affected by winter wet are highly favored.

Overall Beauty

Even if a cultivar has many desirable characteristics, it may not be beautiful. This depends on a year-round appraisal of all aspects of the plant's characteristics. Is the cultivar an improvement over similar cultivars? Would you spend money to purchase this plant? For example, a cultivar might have unique and desirable qualities in several categories, but the overall effect does not work. An example would be a rosette in bright red with good color retention with very thin and few leaves, making for a sparse-looking rosette. Any one of these traits could give a pretty rosette, but not in that combination.

Clump Effect

Part of the charm of semps is their ability to make pretty clumps that can be used as edging in beds, accents in rock gardens, or along dry walls. Because of this, a really good cultivar should make a nice neat clump. When rosettes bloom the clump should fill in quickly, not leave large bare spots. Clumps of large rosettes that have this ability are especially welcome. Cultivars that make excessively long stolons for their increase make sprawling, messy clumps and should be downgraded. A cultivar should make sufficient increase each season that the clump grows at a good rate. Cultivars that produce few increases and/or tend to bloom out should be rated poorly, no matter the beauty.

The Flower and Stalk

In general, semps are not grown for their flowers. However, cultivars with particularly nice flowers can enhance the value of the plant in the landscape. Cultivars with cobwebs and tufts generally have pleasant rose flowers on short stalks. Some cultivars have reddish stalks that contrast with the flowers, making a pleasing effect. For example, I have a *heuffelii* seedling that has very pale bloomstalks with leaves that are bright red and have yellow flowers that make a colorful display. Excessively large stalks that fall over and have insipid flower colors are considered faults. Although most *Sempervivum* flowers are small, cultivars derived from *S. grandiflorum* have a fairly large flower. Some cultivars, especially those derived from *S.*

calcareum, rarely bloom. Some consider this a plus, as there are no messy stalks or chance for stray seedlings.

This is probably the most important criterion. How many of us have heard, "I have the green one?" If you can tell the name of a cultivar in another's garden without looking at the label then the plant is distinct. Even green ones may be distinctive if they have a combination of characteristics that make them unique, such as 'Plastic.' To understand distinction, the hybridizer needs to have a good grasp of the state of the art of hybrids that already exist. We do not need more look-alike cultivars on the market. Asking colleagues with a good knowledge of semp cultivars to evaluate your seedlings honestly is often a help. In fact, I often use two of my local members as a sounding board for a cultivar I am considering marketing. They have brought me back to my senses on a couple of my selections. How I appreciate that! Nothing worse than naming an inferior plant! About one in 1,000 seedlings, even from planned crosses, are distinct enough for the market. The remainder are generally nice plants and can be used for general landscaping projects, especially the red and purple seedlings. One question you might ask in deciding whether a plant should be named is, "would I play $10 for a rosette of this plant?" This makes you think more than once about the worthiness of a cultivar.

WHAT NEXT?

Now that you have your seedling saved and you have determined it is a good plant, what are the next steps? If you are satisfied that your cultivar is worthy of a name, you must find a name that has not been previously used for a semp. There are several sources of cultivar lists that have been maintained by European groups. Until it was disbanded, the Sempervivum Society was designated the official registration authority of cultivar names by the Royal Horticultural Society. They ensured that the name followed the rules of nomenclature for cultivated plant names. Since that time there is no special authority over the genus. The rules are straightforward, though. Good sources of clever names can be found in other plant groups. I have long been a breeder of irises, and many of my early semp names, such as 'Lipstick,' 'Jungle Shadows,' and 'Jungle Fires,' were also names for popular iris cultivars of that era. For a while I had a plant of the border bearded iris 'Jungle Shadows' underplanted with the semp cultivar to show the similar colorations.

There are established rules by which plants are named, and despite not having a society to implement and enforce these rules, the plant you name should be acceptable under these rules. The rules were established to eliminate chaotic naming of plants. Check to make sure the name you have chosen has not been taken by another semp. Both the National Gardening Association and several European websites maintain large lists of cultivar names. Second, find a name that is unlikely to be confused with any others on the list. Follow a few simple rules: no Mr. or Mrs., no use of hyperbole (no "biggest," "reddest"), ensure the name you have chosen will not be confused with another cultivar, get permission for naming plants for people, and stay under three words (although now four words are allowed).

If you are like me, you are never satisfied with your creations, but rather, you look at each as the next step toward an even more perfect semp. As many of my friends know, I want semps that are as big as a football and black. Obviously Rome was not a built in a day, and neither was a foot-wide black cultivar! This year in my seedling patch there are several hundred seedlings from mating 'Heart of Darkness' and 'Borscht.' Both of these cultivars come from a cross of 'Killer' X 'Jungle Shadows,' and both have quite dark colors and are some of the larger cultivars. By crossing these two choice cultivars I obtained a large number of seedlings that are a bit larger than either parent plant and closer to my goal of black. There were also a number of other seedlings that were distinct, such as green and dark purple bicolors and seedlings with odd sorts of watermarks. Although these later types might not get me to my goal, they are certainly saved, and may eventually become the basis for new breeding efforts. That is, when life gives you lemons, you can still make lemonade! My line of blue-leaved hosta started from self-pollinating one of the most handsome variegated cultivars of its day. When all the seedlings turned out blue instead of variegated, that became the new line. Thus, if you have a break in a color or form you had not anticipated, do not be afraid to use it and make those colors or forms a new breeding goal. In crossing some very wide-leaved dark purples, I obtained an incredibly large (twelve inch diameter) silver-leaved plant. This plant was obviously saved and will be a cornerstone of my breeding program for extra-large rosettes.

I tend to cross modern cultivars with modern cultivars, rather than going back to the species, as most species clones are green, or green with purple tips, without much distinction. Many of these species are untapped as far as their genetic potential. It might be interesting to combine some of the more attractive species clones, such as the collections of *S. calcareum* and *S. cantabricum*, with red and purple cultivars.

Most of the hybridizing that has been done in semps are mainly *not* planned crosses, but rather seedlings from open pollinated seed. Thus, it is not surprising that few attempts at line breeding have been tried. Only Nicholas Moore seems to have developed lines from hand crosses, and he was able to produce a number of outstanding cultivars from these efforts. The advantage of line breeding is that interesting recessives can be expressed and results are much more predictable, allowing refinements or intensification of specific traits. For example, since making a cross between 'Jungle Shadows' and 'Killer,' I have taken the best seedlings from this initial cross and then intercrossed the best with each other. By combining these best plants with each other, a number of interesting combinations of the genes from the original parents are now combined in a single individual, including near blacks and black and green bicolors. Interestingly, although both parents have rather narrow leaves, by selecting some of the wider-leaved seedlings to use in crosses some quite wide seedlings were obtained. Conversely, combining some of the narrower-leaved ones have given clones with long, very spidery leaves. Neither of these results would have been obtained through random crosses. As long as these lines stay interesting, I will continue to cross among these extremes and also concentrate on patterns and colors that are unique. Because the original cross of 'Killer' and 'Jungle Shadows' was rather wide (dissimilar parents), the opportunities for producing unique combinations of genetic material are vast. Another line that has a similar diverse genetic base is a cross of 'Lilac Time' and 'Jungle Shadows'—a sort of crazy idea on my part, but one that has netted some very lovely seedlings, including the waterlily-formed blacks I was anticipating, but also really strong pinks and combinations of grey and pink that I had not anticipated. Because these two parent plants are also dissimilar, it is likely that the most interesting plants will come in the next generation, when the siblings from this cross are intercrossed or self-pollinated. In these matings, I crossed the pinkish-toned ones among themselves and the blacks with water lily forms among themselves. These seedlings are now growing in my seedling beds, and it is already evident that many factors, such as rosette size, leaf shape, colors, and patterns are all segregating. Odd combinations of grey, pink, dark purple, and forms from one extreme to another are showing up in the next generation from this mating.

Not everything works out well, however! A cross that was line breeding was 'Helen Payne' and 'Polly Bishop', two sister seedlings from 'Jungle Shadows' X self. Although the seedlings from this group were good, there were only two or three out of 200 that were an advance over their parents. Possibly because the genetic base for this cross was too narrow and the parents chosen were too close in appearance, there was little variation in the seedlings. Further breeding from this line would be unlikely to produce advancements; the line was stale. Some of these seedlings are being combined with unrelated cultivars to start new lines.

Each season I am amazed at things that appear in the seedling patch. I have included photos of some of these interesting seedlings in this chapter. Most will not reach the market, but many will be used as parents to try to bring out the unusual traits that these seedlings possess. For example, among this year's seedlings, there have been numerous examples of ultra-wide leaves, bumps on the leaves, undulating leaves, and absolutely huge (twelve inches plus) rosettes occurring in the patch. These are in addition to interesting changes in color and patterns in the leaves. It is an exciting time to be working with semps. In my first class on hybridizing semps in 2012, I had a large pot of the *Echeveria* hybrid 'Black Knight,' which had huge rosettes of a near black. I jokingly remarked, "My goal is to make a semp with this size and color." In just a couple generations I have. I think that any sort of color, leaf, or rosette form or size is now possible for semps, too. We have examples in other succulent genera to spur us on to create similar effects with semps. Best yet, unlike the tender succulent plants, ours can be grown under normal gardening conditions.

Fig. 7-11. Cherry red *S. heuffelii* seedling.

GENETICS OF *SEMPERVIVUM*

Bill Nixon and I (Vaughn and Nixon 1972) published a paper many years ago in the *Sempervivum Society Journal* as to what was known of the genetics of semps, and although we know a little more now, there has not been a lot of progress in unraveling the genetics of the group, partly because most of the cultivars are from open pollinations, rather than controlled crosses. Unfortunately, bees are rather tight-lipped as to which cultivars they have crossed! Most of the information described below is gathered from my own crosses over the years and the few results from others. I have tried to write this section so that even those without much training in genetics beyond high school biology will have some

◀ **Fig. 7-12.** Frosted purple seedling.

➤ **Fig. 7-13.** Large red/green bicolor seedling.

◀ **Fig. 7-14.** Very furry red seedling.

understanding of the process. Many of our semps are tetraploids, however, and the ratios of traits segregating for dominants and recessives are much more complicated than in the diploid plants, which is what Mendel described in peas. In the concluding sections of this chapter I will include some of this more technical information for those who want to delve a bit deeper into the subject. Those not trained in some genetics may want to consult with some elementary genetics texts.

Color of the Rosette

We are lucky that the presence of red or purple color due to anthocyanin pigments seems to be dominant to the prevailing green color that is found in so many of our semp species. It was the rare varieties found in the field, such as 'Rubrum' clone of *S. montanum* and the reddish forms of *tectorum* and *marmoreum*, that gave rise to all of our color variants in the other species. So if we cross a red or purple cultivar on to a green one, most of the seedlings are red or purple. In some cases, the color distribution is changed in these crosses. For example, some crosses of green X red give not completely red cultivars, but rather those with red just at the base or toward the top of the leaves. These sorts of results may mean that the other parent contains genes that control the distribution of anthocyanin that results in a different distribution than is found in the all purple or all red parent. In crosses between all purple cultivars and these bicolors, most of the seedlings have been bicolors, indicating that this regulation of anthocyanin distribution trait is due to dominant gene(s). Some of these bicolors have just the smallest amount of anthocyanin at the leaf bases, whereas others leave only the tips of the leaves green and the remainder of the rosette red or purple. In many ways these are some of the most striking cultivars.

In the *heuffelii* cultivars, red or purple is also dominant to green. Because this species is a simple diploid, one can see the rather classic Mendelian ratios of 3:1 red:green very clearly in the second generation from self-pollinating one of these red from red X green parents. Nice to have some that behave like Mendel's peas! Many other semps are tetraploids, and that 3:1 ratio becomes 35:1 in tetraploids (see following).

Yellow in the *heuffelii* cultivars also behaves as a recessive. Here is Ed Skrocki's story of how the yellows came about:

> One plant that came from the old Correvon Gardens in Switzerland, an
> old time plant nursery in the 1950s and '60s, was *J. heuffelii* 'Kapanoikense'
> [This clone was different than one subsequently listed by Peter Mitchell

with this same name]. It blooms heavily and has lots of flowers. When that flat of seeds germinated an amazing thing happened. A few plants were sulfur yellow. Now there was a brand new color in this plant strain. I gave the new yellow ones tender loving care, so as not to lose a single one. Luckily, I did not lose any and had about five plants grown to full size. Now I considered myself to be a full-fledged nurseryman, and many people came to see my very large collection. (Skrocki 2003)

From these seedlings the cultivars 'Xanthoheuff,' 'Lemon Sky,' and 'Gold Bug' were selected for introduction. Ed further speculated that his yellows were due to intercrosses with the roller types. We know this not to be true, as such hybrids are sterile or nearly so, but rather, what he did was uncover the recessives, and also allow bees to create combinations of genetic material that were not present in the clones that were collected in the wild because of the geographic separation. Bringing them all together unleashed these possibilities. Crosses of yellows, such as 'Orange Tip' with green ones, gives all green progeny, although the genetics of the newer gold clones of semps has not been tested to my knowledge. The new 'Cheese' series plants are a mix of seed from the existing gold ones, such as 'Orange Tip,' 'Xanthoheuff,' and 'Gold Bug,' although the 'Cheese' series is from open-pollinated seed.

Flower color behaves similarly to rosette colors. Red color is dominant to white or yellow flowers, although you can often see patches of yellow color on flowers that are hybrids from red flower X yellow flower crosses (Zonneveld 1980), or the flowers are an odd shade of pink. I often use those cultivars with odd-colored flowers in my breeding, knowing that they are themselves a cross of two dissimilar types and have a greater chance of producing unusual progeny.

Leaf Texture and Hairs

Leaf texture varies from smooth and shiny, satiny because of surface waxes, velvety because of dense hairs, and leaves edged with cilia. All of these can add distinction and interest to these hybrids.

Velvety leaves are dominant to smooth ones, so it is easily possible to create velvety cultivars with all the colors and patterns found in the glabrous cultivars by crossing with them. For example, the cross of the velvety 'Cleveland Morgan' with *S. calcareum* gave rise to the velvety hybrid 'Greenwich Time.' The presence of the velvet causes a darker or more somber leaf color, as well.

When cobwebbed semps are crossed to non-cobwebs, the first generation seedlings do not have a full cobweb, but tufts of hairs at the leaf terminus. Arends was the first to demonstrate this phenomenon when he crossed S. arachnoideum with S. tectorum and obtained the tufted hybrids 'Alpha' and 'Beta.' It has been repeated many times in the garden and in the wild, too. There are almost endless possibilities of combining these charming tufts with all sorts of leaf textures, sizes, and colors. To me, the tufted types are one of the most interesting groups. Prolific hybridizer Ed Skrocki focused almost entirely on this group and the cobwebs toward the end of his hybridizing career. They combine the very neat habit and vigor of the cobwebs, the tuft of hair, and the unique characteristics from the other parent. The only problem with this group is the limited fertility of some of these plants, many with only less than five percent functional pollen. However, there are many easily fertile ones that can be used to get a second (or later) generation of seedlings. The extent of cobwebbing in the second generation varies from complete to tiny tufts of hair at the leaf tips, or more rarely no tuft at all.

The presence of cilia along the leaf edges adds an interesting sort of silvered effect to the leaf edges in cultivars that have these cilia. The presence of these leaf edge cilia also appears to be dominant over the absence of cilia, although sometimes the progeny from ciliated X non-ciliated forms have less cilia than the ciliated parent.

Rosette Size and Leaf Shape

Size of the rosettes, the density of leaves, and the shapes of leaves are under the control of many genes, so hybrids between different types of plants will often give hybrids intermediate in character between the two parents. For example, in crosses between the small cobwebs and bigger non-cobwebs, the rosettes are bigger than the cobweb parent but smaller than the non-cobweb parent. These progeny tend toward the smaller side, rather than exactly in between, indicating that several of the genes for smallness from the cobweb parent are dominant for this trait. When these tufted intermediate types are self-pollinated, the progeny show a greater size range, some as small as the cobweb parent, but rarely as big as the larger non-cobweb parent. For example, the self-pollination of the tufted hybrid 'Fluffy Fluke' gave rosettes that ranged in size from ½ in. to over four inches in diameter. Likewise, leaf shape is controlled by a number of genes, and crosses between divergent leaf shapes give rise to a wide range of leaf shapes. In my lines I have been selecting for excessively broad leaves, and it has been possible to get leaves of exceptional width, although generally these plants also have far fewer leaves, as though they are compensating for the lack of leaves by increasing their width.

Mark Smith, Favarger, and colleagues (1968) made crosses between nearly all of the species of *Sempervivum*, and in almost all cases it was possible to make such crosses. Considering the wide range of chromosome counts in these species (from 38 to 108), that is a most amazing occurrence and gives the hybridizer the chance to explore genes from a variety of species. The most difficult of these crosses are between *heuffelii* and *globiferum* with any of the non-*Jovibarba* semps (Hatch 1984; Zonneveld 1985). These crosses result in few progeny, and the progeny often have an abnormal morphology and are completely sterile (Hatch 1984).

In the crosses between other types of semps, the fertility of the hybrids depends on the chromosome counts of the parents (Zonneveld 1982). *Sempervivum* species may either be diploid, with two sets of chromosomes, or tetraploid, with four sets of chromosomes. Some species, such as *S. arachnoideum*, occur in diploid and tetraploid forms. When a diploid species goes into meiosis it contributes one set of chromosomes to the progeny. In a cross with another diploid species, the one set of chromosomes from each species works in producing a viable normal offspring. There are many examples of such hybrids, and these are often fine garden plants, such as 'Greenwich Time,' which has a diploid set from a *montanum* and another set from *calcareum*. We can diagram this cross as *montanum* (MM) X *calcareum* (CC), resulting in the hybrid (MC). The problem with the diploid X diploid hybrids happens in meiosis, as male and female gametes are produced. Each chromosome needs an exact match to pair so that good pollen cells and ovules are formed. Because the two species contribute different chromosomes (or even different numbers of chromosomes), the chromosomes do not pair easily or at all, resulting in pollen cells with odd numbers of chromosomes that are mostly aborted. Despite these problems, the plant is still able to produce around five percent viable pollen and a few seeds, especially if allowed to be open pollinated by more fertile semps. Considering you are crossing the plant equivalent of a mule, it is amazing that they are this fertile! Hybrids such as these are apt to give you few seedlings even from open pollination, and I have never gotten seedlings from 'Greenwich Time,' 'Aymon Correvon,' or 'Purdy's 90-1,' and not for lack of trying! The pollen on flowers of 'Greenwich Time' are an odd shade of lemon, not the much darker golden color one observes in fully fertile plants. This is a clue that your plant is not fertile, or at least is nearly pollen sterile.

Crosses of diploid plants with tetraploid plants produce triploid plants, with one set of chromosomes from the diploid parent and two sets from the tetraploid parent. Examples of this type of hybrid are the two Arends hybrids 'Alpha' and 'Beta,' which are crosses of a diploid *arachnoideum* (AA) and a tetraploid *tectorum* (TTTT), resulting in hybrids of constitution

ATT. In these hybrids, the chromosomes of the tetraploid parent pair with each other during meiosis and a random number from the diploid parent are incorporated into each pollen cell or ovule. These hybrids can have a quite respectable percentage of good pollen—roughly fifty percent in many cases, although I have found this very variable from cultivar to cultivar and dependent upon how related the two parental species are. It is not known how many chromosomes of the diploid parent are passed along, although the tufted hybrids from diploid *arachnoideum* often produce tufted progeny, indicating that at least those chromosomes associated with terminal hair production are included in gametes. Certainly one expects at least a full set of the T genome to be included in the sex cells, as these chromosomes have a partner and should be passed on in pollen and ovules with little problem.

The most fertile of the hybrids are when tetraploid species are crossed with tetraploid species. It is difficult to tell tetraploids from diploids in the semps, as the normal morphological markers for tetraploids (larger size chiefly) do not always hold for rosette size. Blossom size is a better indicator, with tetraploid flowers about forty percent bigger than the corresponding diploid. By using the basic (haploid) number 16-19, you can determine whether your species is a diploid or a tetraploid. Some species also have diploid and tetraploid strains. For example, there are tetraploid strains of *S. arachnoideum* which are no bigger than the diploids, although the tetraploids tend to be larger. Crossing these tetraploid strains of *arachnoideum* (AAAA) with tetraploid strains of *tectorum* (TTTT) gives rise to hybrids with full sets of chromosomes from each parent (AATT). Every chromosome has a pairing partner and the pollen cells have a balanced number of chromosomes (AT); the percentage of normal pollen is nearly 100%. The only problem with these hybrids is trying to get hybrids that differ from these plants, as the genes are in stabilized complexes, so the genes do not segregate. That is, the two diploid sets (AA and TT) stay the same, with no interchange of material between the chromosomes. Self-pollination of these tetraploid hybrids results in many nearly identical plants. This can be as frustrating as a near sterile plant for the hybridizer trying to produce improved forms. The trick here is to cross to plants with similar genetic constitution but different parents so that new combinations of genes are introduced into the crosses.

Conclusions

Growing semps from seed and creating new hybrids can be a fun hobby, and it is more than a little addicting. Even though most of the seedlings will represent no improvement over existing cultivars, there are almost always a few special ones that are worth carrying on for further breeding. Others can be used for general landscaping or potting projects where named cultivars are not needed. The excitement of finding something really special and different is what drives most of us to keep crossing and rowing out ridiculous numbers of seedlings. As I was finishing this chapter, I came across a poem written by iris hybridizer Walker Ferguson entitled "Flower Hybridizer" (1962). The reference to "beards" refers to these structures on the falls of bearded irises, but the remainder of the poem can refer to *any* flower breeder. We are all dreamers, and we want what we do not have already. As a person trying to develop a football-sized semp in jet black, this poem seemed like an especially appropriate end.

Fig. 7-15. An exotically colored seedling of Beatrix Bodmeier's.

THE FLOWER HYBRIDIZER

Some people are happy to grow what there is,
But we want to grow what there ain't.
If we've ever seen it, it's surely no good;
It should be quite different or quaint.
Now a blue dandelion might look pretty nice,
Or a daffodil, sucking its thumb.
Those common old things as they always have been
Are only for folks who are dumb.
If beards come in yellow, we wish they were black,
Or if they are black, we want red.
We just can't tolerate things as they are.
Do let us have something instead.
The bright shining stars of a few years ago

Are now completely passé,

It's hard to imagine how anyone could

Consider them charming or gay.

A white marigold has been greatly desired,

As well as a yellow sweet pea.

The reason is simple. As far as we know,

Those colors don't happen to be,

The things that are short, we strive to make tall,

Those naturally large we develop in small.

This is listed as progress, but progress to what?

The progress is only what we ain't got!

REFERENCES

Favarger C et al. (1968) "Hybrides interspecifiques et intergenerique chez les Joubarbes." Arch. Julius Klaus-Stiftung Vererbungsf. 43: 18–30 (A translated version is available in the *Sempervivum Society Journal.*)

Ferguson W (1962) *The Flower Hybridizer.* Bull Amer Iris Soc 166:75

Hatch LC (1984) "Vegetative anomalies in controlled intrageneric (Sempervivum X Sempervivum) and intergeneric (Sempervivum X Jovibarba) crosses." *Sempervivum Fanciers Association Newsletter* 10(2): 7–10

Mitchell M (1976) "The art of hybridizing." *Sempervivum Society Journal* 7 (1): 3-6

Skrocki E (2003) "*Sempervivum* and *Orystachys* seed harvesting and planting." *Winter Hardy Cactus & Succulent Association* 3(1): 10-12

Smith M (1971) "Sempervivum hybrids." *Sempervivum Society Journal* 2: 2–5

Smith M (1979) "*Sempervivum* germination trials." *Sempervivum Society Journal* 10(1); 30-32

Vaughn KC, Nixon CW (1972) "Genetic considerations in the Sempervivum group." *Sempervivum Society Journal*

Zonneveld BJM (1980) "A method for recognizing a yellow-flowered parent in a reddish-flowered hybrid Sempervivum." *Sempervivum Fanciers Association Newsletter* 6(1): 5

Zonneveld BJM (1982) "A simple method to test the hybridity of Sempervivum." *Sempervivum Fanciers Association Newsletter* 8(2):9

Zonneveld BJM (1985) "X Jovium Rowley." *Sempervivum Fanciers Association Newsletter* 11(2): 7

CHAPTER 8

PEOPLE THAT HELPED DEVELOP OR PROMOTE SEMPERVIVUM

The current state of semps has not come about without the hand of man. Whereas the wild species were mostly green or had drab colors, the semps presently on the market offer a bewildering array of colors, forms, sizes, and textures. This did not happen overnight, but rather, people all over the world contributed to this effort. It is an amazing story of chance contacts, devoted workers, and scientific study all melded into developing these plants into their present state. Even this chapter gives just a fraction of the people responsible for this revolution. It has been my privilege to have either met or corresponded with many of them. Many of these people are extraordinary in their lives beyond semps, too. I think you will find these stories fascinating.

NORTH AMERICAN HYBRIDIZERS

Carl Purdy

Carl Purdy was a revolution in California horticulture. He was one of the first to realize the value of many of the native plants of California and set up a nursery in Ukiah, California, that specialized in these treasures and introduced them around the world. Although Purdy was not formally educated, he was respected by many academics and has several species named in his honor. The 1939 American Iris Checklist (Peckham 1940) describes him as, "collector of native plants for 60 years, lecturing, writing, and gardening nearly as long. Author of monographs on *Calochortus* and Indian basketry." Clearly Purdy was quite a Renaissance man. He was a voracious reader, and obviously had a wonderful sense of business, as well as

CARL PURDY, JAN., 1901.

◀ ▼ **Fig. 8-1.** Carl Purdy portrait and 'Purdy's 90-1,' a lovely velvety grey that is a frustrating parent.

an innate understanding of plants. Purdy was a close confidant of legendary breeder Luther Burbank (Shinn et al. 1901). Famed Swiss Alpine garden specialist Henri Correvon traveled to Ukiah, California, to visit with Purdy. Although the two were unable to communicate (other than in the Latin names of plants!), Correvon sent a complete collection of his *Sempervivum* collection to Purdy, thus ensuring their distribution in the US.

Here is a bit from Purdy's book *My Life and My Times* (published thirty years after his death in 1976) that shows a bit of the pragmatism of this breeder in doing work with semps:

> Very soon a rock-garden section was included in my catalogs. The *Sempervivum*, commonly called hen-and-chickens, was a plant eminently fitted to rock gardening, and sensing the coming fad, I began to build a collection of them. Very soon, where no other dealer had more than a few, I had dozens, and by getting them from every possible source, including large importations of European collections, I soon had over 300 named sorts. I distributed widely and profitably, but like irises, they are too easy, and in a few years were in every little nursery. One has to keep moving to be in the van in horticultural progress.

He acknowledges Clarence Lown (of semp hybrid 'Lown's 60,' a tufted type) as being instrumental to his interest in semps. Lown had one of the first rock gardens in the US at his estate in Poughkeepsie, New York, and was an unabashed promoter of rock gardens. When Purdy saw the popularity of this movement he capitalized on it.

Oddly, Purdy does not mention any of his hybridizing in *My Life and Times*. When I first started breeding semps in 1964, his 'Purdy's 70-40,' 'Purdy's 50-5,' and 'Purdy's 90-1' were among the finest cultivars available. 'Purdy's 50-5' was the parent of my first introduction, 'Silvertone,' and I am still using the other two in crosses. Since that time a cultivar known as 'Purdy's Big Red' has appeared and was distributed by Ed Skrocki. All of these were marketed after Carl Purdy's death, so I imagine any pedigree information is also long lost. Considering he had imported many of the fine European varieties, he started with fine breeding stock and put the production of American hybrids on firm ground for future hybridizers.

F. Cleveland Morgan

F. Cleveland Morgan was a man of many talents. After formal education in England and Canada, he ran a family business that owned a number of stores across Canada. These were later sold to the Hudson Bay Company. These stores were the source of funds that enabled Cleveland Morgan to pursue his interest in art and gardening. He was an early proponent of the rock garden, and his Montreal rock garden was second to none. It was in this rock garden that an amazing collection of semps was housed. Among these plants appeared a seedling named 'Cleveland Morgan,' a very round and dark red with velvety leaves. For many years it was the top variety in its class and was a favorite of Sandy MacPherson. It also was an outstanding parent, producing high quality seedlings almost invariably. Moreover, for a velvety cultivar, it suffered almost no damage from moisture that seemed to ruin other cultivars.

Besides semps, Cleveland Morgan also hybridized Siberian irises, and his 'Caesar's Brother' is probably the most planted Siberian iris in the world. It is behind almost every dark-flowered Siberian iris on the market. For his hybridizing efforts, the American Iris Society awarded him the Hybridizers Medal and the award for the best Siberian iris is named in his honor.

Edward Skrocki

Edward Skrocki, affectionately known as "Eddy," is our most prolific US hybridizer, and for years he almost single-handedly made the American semp hybrids the most sought after cultivars in the world. He is credited with originating over 200 different cultivars, with many winning awards from the Sempervivum Society. Like many of us, Ed's first order of semp plants was from Sandy MacPherson in the early '60s, and he soon had all the plants that

Sandy offered (Mentgen 1993a). He started growing semp seedlings in the late '60s, and when we first made contact in 1969, he had already selected a number of seedlings. Ed did not hybridize per se, but he gathered all of his seed that was generated by open pollination by insects and simply harvested it into a huge shoe box (he eventually used a more secure metal container!). These were planted out, and sometimes 20,000 seedlings were produced in a given year. This method (dubbed the "Skrocki method") worked well for him, but most people would not have time (and the patience) to row out that many seedlings in a given year (or a lifetime!). With these random matings between so many cultivars, Ed was able to select for a number of very unique and distinctive cultivars and pushed the boundaries of what semps were in color, size, shape, and pattern. In addition to using this seed for the production of his own seedlings, Ed sold seed to Park and Thompson and Morgan seed companies. That seed, designated "American Hybrids" in the T&M catalog, was sold around the world, and no doubt made for a number of semp enthusiasts. Ed did occasionally separate out seed from special cultivars that he wanted to grow on from a particular female parent, even though the seed was open pollinated, so some of his cultivars do have known pod parents.

Ed produced many outstanding hybrids, and his cultivars won numerous Awards of Merit and Rosette Awards from the Sempervivum Society, including awards for 'Xanthoheuff,' 'Olivette,' and 'Ohio Burgundy.' In the latter half of his breeding career he focused on the cobweb and tufted groups, feeling that these were the most interesting groups and the most variable from seed. From these efforts he produced such outstanding cultivars as 'Fluffy Fluke,' 'Lively Bug,' and 'Butterfly.' He described 'Fluffy Fluke' as his favorite cultivar of his own raising (Mentgen 1993a). Another of his important contributions was to pull out the yellow color in the all-green *S. heuffelii* 'Kaponikense,' and from it he produced 'Xanthoheuff,' 'Lemon Sky,' and 'Gold Bug,' all of which are still widely grown. Moreover, these served as parents for the next generation of yellow cultivars. Many of the other outstanding cultivars developed by Ed are covered in the cultivar chapter. Growers will not be disappointed by growing any of these.

Ed's hybrids were introduced by Oakhill Gardens and the Perennial Gardens and sold throughout the world. Ed himself started selling plants out of a retail nursery and ran it for several years when he became a wholesale only nursery, as dealing with customers became too great for him to handle. In addition to his work with semps and sedums, Ed worked with hosta as well, introducing 'Cadillac,' 'Lime Regis,' and 'Patrician.' He was always amused that hosta prices were so inflated compared to semps, where prices of $200 for a new introduction were not uncommon. Much more than the few dollars that a new semp might bring!

Fig. 8-2. Ed Skrocki's letterhead

Ed was a character in all aspects of his life, and he had "collectivitis" not just for semps, but also for other objects. He had an impressive collection of Packard automobiles and sold Packard parts to other enthusiasts. His huge hybrid 'Packardian' was named to honor these automobiles. Later, he became a huge collector of matchbooks, and these also became a mini-business effort. You have to admire his ability to turn his hobbies into other careers. It makes "working" so much easier when you have a passion for your job.

One of the trademarks of his nursery was his most unusual method for transport of plants: a hearse! Ed could load many stacks of trays into the back of the hearse and would deliver his plants in the hearse. I am sure this raised more than a few eyebrows or caused some concerns of death when the hearse arrived! This was just an example of Ed's devilish sense of humor. Both he and his hybrids will be long remembered. I remember one call when he attempted to get Helen Payne to raise our compensation on our hybrids. He succeeded, and we all got a little money for our originations, not just the fame of appearing in Helen's catalog!

Ed's desire to collect all the semps that were available led him to exchange plants with growers in Europe. Because it was illegal to ship plants without permits, Ed devised a unique system to thwart the authorities. He bought large tubes used to mail newspapers and then stuffed a number of semps into the center of the tube, then cut ends of a *Cleveland Plain Dealer* newspaper, making it appear that it was *all* newspaper should any official care to look. I am *not* recommending this as a practice!

Ed passed away on March 23, 2010, after leading a very full life devoted to semps.

Polly Bishop

Pauline Sears Bishop, known to everyone as Polly, was my mentor in this field. When I first saw her Athol, Massachusetts, garden in 1964, she had virtually every semp available in the US. Her garden was unique, with paths sunken into the ground that were bordered by stone walls, with semps spilling out from the beds all the way into the paths. Her sandy soil was just perfect for semp culture, and the plants grew to large sizes and formed large clumps. Before starting to breed semps, Polly had extensive experience breeding irises and daylilies. Polly became frustrated with the few seeds that were produced from each hand cross. She decided to take bloomstalks of all the dark purple cultivars in a crisscross pattern and allow bees to cross all the flowers, then planted all the seed from these bloomstalks. The logic of this was that we really did not know what genes were controlling dark rosettes color, so all matings should be made. From these random matings between the dark cultivars she raised several hundred seedlings, pulling out all the green ones and allowing the darkest purple ones to develop. From this group Polly selected 'Dark Cloud' and 'Plumb Rose' (see cultivar list for descriptions), but there were several dozen very fine plants that were much darker than other plants of that era. Polly was very critical of seedlings being named that were not worthy, and she only introduced one other, 'Pink Lemonade,' which is from open-pollinated seed of 'Magnificum.' She considered 'Magnificum' one of the best of the semps of that era and grew both open pollinated seed and made crosses with this cultivar. Her philosophy of only selecting a few that should be named is a good one, as her plants are still grown around the world forty years after they were marketed by Betty Bronow in her *The Perennial Gardens* catalog. Polly gardened into her '90s and maintained a huge collection of semps.

Pat Warner nee Drown

Patricia (Drown) Warner started crossing under Polly Bishop's tutelage as a child (see preface). Pat planted several gardens of semps with rocks scattered like an outcropping, and with semps planted artistically throughout. Her most famous cultivar from her breeding is 'Missouri Rose,' which has outstanding deep rose-purple color that intensifies during the season and is one of the few in this color range that looks good in August each year. This was one of several pinkish seedlings that came up spontaneously. It was originally named 'Wine and Roses,' but Mennonite Helen Payne changed the named to 'Missouri Rose,' not wanting to glamorize drinking alcohol! 'Tamberlane' (we think Helen *meant* 'Tamerlane,' but this was how it was initially listed) was also renamed by Helen, as she thought the original name 'Green and Purple Velvet' was too narrow a description of the plant. Pat was trying for a velvety version of 'Sanford Hybrid,' but 'Tamberlane' is really quite a bit more. In the spring it has rusty brown color, but the rosette transforms into a very incurved rosette, with the deep purple tips of the leaves forming a deep center—very unique. Pat obtained a degree in marine biology from the University of Massachusetts Dartmouth, then headed to Seattle to obtain a degree in aerospace engineering from the University of Washington. She has worked in the aerospace industry in the Seattle area since then.

Pat's father raised and bred Siberian huskies. Three of the names of her introductions—'Kanno's Cobweb,' 'Little Tisha,' and 'Neoga's Delight'—are names in honor of three of her dad's best breeding females. Her 'Denise's Cobweb' is named for her sister.

Mina Colvin

Mina Colvin lived in Nashville, Indiana, a beautiful area of Brown County with rolling hills and beautiful fall foliage that draws people from all over the Midwest. In this lovely backdrop Mina Colvin created a large rock garden. An order to Helen Payne for sedums included a couple semps and Mina was hooked. A trip to Oregon to visit Helen Payne sealed the deal for Mina; she was a sempaholic now! These visits were even recorded in Helen's book:

> For example, a customer and friend, from Indiana, has visited us twice, each
> time bringing us something of interest from her state. The phone company must
> love us, as we have had many other visits by phone. (Payne 1972)

Of course those were the days long before cell phones when long distance calls were pricey.

Mina's favorite semp was *S. arachnoideum* 'Tomentosum,' and she was curious about the seed raising process and collected open-pollinated seed from that plant. From that seed she raised two outstanding semps: raspberry red 'Raspberry Ice' and silvery grey 'Silver Thaw.' Both plants have very prominent cilia and are neat growers. 'Raspberry Ice' won a Silver Rosette from the Sempervivum Society. One of her other hybrids that I think is quite nice is 'Viking,' a dark purple with nice shape and copious watermarks that make for season-long interest.

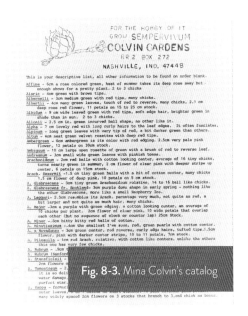

Fig. 8-3. Mina Colvin's catalog

For a while Mina also sold plants as a retail nursery. She also did a lot of work with native phlox species, and her white cultivar of *Phlox bifida* 'Colvin's White' is sold by many nurseries—a wonderful ground cover plant for shade. This was a seedling that she discovered in her yard that had much wider petals than other white forms of this species.

Gary Gossett

Gary Gossett was another early starter at the semp game, and he was one of the members of the round robin that served as the nucleus for the Sempervivum Fanciers Association. A degree in business from the University of Chicago made him a savvy marketer, as well. His trademark 'Pacific' series was a stroke of marketing genius. He was the first to create a "stable" name for his hybrids, so that it would be immediately obvious that a plant was a result of his crossing. This is an outstanding series of plants, and many of these cultivars are described in further detail in the cultivar section. I have grown and used many of these cultivars in my own breeding program. 'Pacific Spring Frost' and 'Pacific Jordan' are my two favorites at this time, but you can't go wrong with any of these.

In a recent phone call from Gary, he describes himself as a great selector of plants rather than as a hybridizer. Gary was clever in using bees to his advantage. He cut all the bloomstalks off of any green cultivar so that only the red and purple cultivars were available to be crossed and he grouped the *heuffelii* types. He described his process in detail in a *Sempervivum Fanciers Association Newsletter* (1985), and I have printed it in its entirety so you can see how the Pacific strain was developed:

> **Question:** Hybridizing without certainty—To be seed or not to be seed: that is the question. (Bill Nixon notes here, "Forgive us, Mr. Shakespeare.")

> **Answer:** The benefits of planting bee seed are that you get lots of seed and this can select out the more extreme forms for further growing. Thus, if properly managed, growing open-pollinated (bee) seed allows many new hybrids to be produced for evaluation.

> I make it a practice to encourage self-crossing for about the first thousand seedlings from a clone. This can essentially be achieved by simply grouping several bloomers together in an area removed from other blooming stalks and let the bees go at it. Seeing the full range of variability allows me to select out extremes that are like the parent but better. It also brings many recessive traits out into the open. It allows one to "make book" on which plants tend to have lots of highly colored seedlings and/or seedlings with good form.

> After I have a reasonably extreme form of any line/group, it is time to see how well it crosses with other kinds. I place the bloomers near others that were different enough to make new different hybrids. All bloomers for outcrossing are placed in

▲ **Fig. 8-4.** 'Pacific Devil's Food'

◀ **Fig. 8-5.** 'Pacific Spring Frost'

an area of 20 feet × 20 feet. This encourages bees to spend lots of time in that one area so that much outcrossing occurs. *J. heuffelii*'s are kept together since a longer-tongued bumblebee seems to specialize in these. Most semps, however, are serviced by honey bees.

Sooner or later, there are specific crosses I want to see made. I mix a group of such plants together and go out and rub my finger from flower to flower (a brush would likely be better). Up to 40% hybridization rates have been achieved here via this method. The drawback of such open pollination is that you do not know for certain the parents of any hybrid. On the other hand, I soon get good at guessing after seeing the next generation.

Be warned that, if you want to play the percentages and use bee seed, you are assuring yourself of thousands of seeds that will need sowing, watering, shading, transplanting, and getting rid of. For sure, the vast majority of such seedlings are boring or else duplicates of named plants. In general, the 99% rule holds: 99% of all seedlings should be tossed out before they get old enough to flower. This year, I raised 30,000 seedlings and perhaps 30 will be good enough for distribution and/ or future work. The only way to get a few good seedlings is to grow lots of seeds.

So Gary got bees to do much of his work by eliminating potentially uninteresting matings and increasing his odds that they would cross varieties that he wanted to use. It is sort of a variation on the technique that Polly Bishop used to create her dark semps, but on a much larger scale. As he notes at the end of his remarks, hybridizing plants is a numbers game, too: the more you grow, the better your chances are of finding a good plant. Later, he developed a relationship with Squaw Mountain Gardens and would stop by several times a year to evaluate plants and collect seeds for his breeding program. Squaw Mountain Gardens would introduce these latter hybrids to the market.

I think everyone would agree that Gary's Pacific series is a wonderful group of plants and ones that will be treasured for a long time.

Gary has had several high-power jobs in the horticulture industry, including as the garden marketing director for the Fred Meyer Company and as breeder of succulents for Terra Nova, one of the largest perennial suppliers in the world. Through these jobs he has greatly influenced horticulture in the US.

Emma Elliott (Wild Ginger Farms)

Emma Elliott and Truls Jensen run the amazing Wild Ginger Farm nursery in Oregon that concentrates on rock garden plants, US West Coast native plants, and other rare garden gems. The property is beautifully landscaped and features ways in which the home gardener can use these plants. Emma has also introduced a number of semp cultivars. Some of my favorites are the large pale violet-tinged blue 'Aqua,' bright red-green bicolor 'Harlequin Rouge,' and the very prolific chocolate brown 'Hot Cocoa.' Not many breeders are working with the cobweb types, but Emma introduced two good (and very prolific) ones: 'Spinner' (great name, wish I had thought of it!) and 'Rosa Spumonti.' These were all grown from a mixture of open pollinated seed, similar to the way in which Ed Skrocki grew his seedlings. Although Wild Ginger Farm sold through mail order, business demands have forced them to limit sales to on premise or through garden sale events in the Pacific Northwest. Luckily, many of these cultivars have been distributed and should be available from other sources, too.

Fig. 8-6. 'Borscht'

Kevin Vaughn

I started hybridizing in 1964, under the tutelage of Polly Bishop, and have been hybridizing something ever since (see the preface). My first introduction was the silver with pink leaf tips 'Silvertone,' but my first really outstanding semps were the large and dark blend 'Jungle Shadows' and the velvety brick red 'Lipstick.' I was not alone in my opinion of these plants, as 'Jungle Shadows' won a Silver Rosette and 'Lipstick' won a Bronze Rosette from the Sempervivum Society, although I would have rated them in reverse order. They were also very big sellers for Helen, and nearly fifty years after their introduction both are still grown around the world. About eighty cultivars were selected and introduced from the first phase of my hybridizing career as a kid in Massachusetts. My parents maintained my rock garden and semp collection while I was in graduate school. Plants of anything that appeared interesting were sent to Helen Payne when I was home to observe the plants, and many of these plants were eventually marketed.

This interest in the genetic aspects of plants led to a PhD in botany with a specialty in genetics. My PhD was on the inheritance of variegation in hosta, with most of the plants used in my research coming from my breeding program that I started on my parents' property. For thirty years I worked for the USDA in Stoneville, Mississippi, investigating various aspects of plant cell biology, many centering on aspects of weed biology, herbicide resistance, and mode of action. Although semps were difficult to grow in Mississippi, I hybridized iris, tradescantia, hosta, daffodils, and daylilies, and introduced many cultivars to the market. Several of these cultivars have won national awards, including the DeBaillon Medal for my iris 'Red Velvet Elvis.' Upon retiring in 2010, I moved to Salem, Oregon, not far from where Helen Payne distributed my hybrids to the world, and have gotten back many of the plants of my youth, as well as obtained breeding stock from around the world. The semp hybridizing has continued at a new high level here, with up to 6,000 seedlings evaluated each year. 'Jungle Shadows' has proven to be a fine parent in my rekindled hybridizing program in Oregon, and I am now on the F2 and F3 of the seedlings from my crosses here. Many of these new cultivars are described in the cultivar section.

Nothing with pollen is safe in my yard, as I am now hybridizing virtually all types of iris, daffodils, hostas, penstemons, hardy geraniums, heleniums, alliums, asters, and daylilies, among some of the more prominent projects. With this variety of plants I get to see something new that I have created virtually each day.

Since 2012, I have organized a Hybridizing Clinic through the National Gardening Association chat group that features tours of local gardens and a class in my garden on the finer points of growing and selecting seedlings. The class is followed by a banquet at a local eatery. Everyone goes home smarter and happier! Interest is clearly growing in these plants by the number of attendees and activity at the National Gardening Association chat group.

EUROPEAN HYBRIDIZERS

It is not surprising that some of the first serious work on semps was carried out in Europe. They grow in the wild there and had been used for centuries as roof adornments and medicinally. Moreover, keen-eyed horticulturalists were quick to pick out unique clones of a species or hybrids that occurred in nature. With these plants in their hands further work, primarily in Britain, the Netherlands, Belgium, and Germany, were critical in elevating semps to their present state of development. The German hybridizers have some of the finest hybrids now on the market. Many of these plants have not reached the US market, although now that interactions between semp enthusiasts on both continents are strengthening, a number of these cultivars are becoming available here in the US. Conversely, some of the best American hybrids are now being sold in Europe, too.

Georg Arends

German Georg Arends was the one who really showed that semps could be improved by breeding. He made a cross of S. *arachnoideum* and S. *tectorum* and obtained three great hybrids named 'Alpha,' 'Beta,' and 'Gamma.' These three hybrids illustrate dramatically the principal that cobweb X non-cobweb crossed gives plants with tufts of hair on each leaf, but not a full cobweb. Even though they were introduced in 1927, they are still available today as a measure of their quality. 'Beta' I find the most interesting, as it is rather atypical of this type of cross, having more narrow leaves and being smaller and more brightly colored than many first generation *arachnoideum* X *tectorum* type of cross.

Even though Arends only introduced three semp hybrids, he was a most prolific perennial hybridizer, introducing over 350 cultivars to the market. Famed perennial plant breeder Alan Bloom (1991) described Arend's work: "I would say that no other continental hardy-plant nursery has developed and distributed so many hybrids of value in so wide a range."

Because of the severe climate in which he gardened, his plants are hardy even in the most difficult climates. Arend's work with astilbe, azaleas, rhododendrons, phlox, and bergenia are still a part of every garden, even though he passed away in 1952. His hosta hybrid *H. sieboldiana* 'Elegans' is the basis of my blue line and many others. We have much to thank Arends for his outstanding breeding work. One has to consider how many times the wonderful sedum *Hylotelephium* 'Autumn Joy' ('Herbstfreude') is used in landscapes all over the world to get a measure of his impact on the horticultural world—probably the most used succulent on the planet. Quite a legacy!

Henri Correvon

Henri Correvon was a man way ahead of his time. He was alarmed when he saw the indiscriminate collecting of Alpine plants for sale in the markets of the lowlands and knew that it was not sustainable. Along with fellow semp enthusiast Edmond Boissier, he founded the Society for the Protection of Alpine Plants. Although he did collect specimens from the mountains, what he sold were plants that had been propagated in his nursery. Besides his work with semps, he is also well known for his work with *Campanula*. He published a series of definitive articles on these plants in *The Garden*.

Correvon was the first to author what one might consider a monograph on the genus, *Les Joubarbes* (1929), although Correvon was quick to say this was *not* a monograph, and hinted that botanists were working on one. Because Correvon was associated with botanists and botanical gardens, he received plants from a number of sources and used these names religiously. Unfortunately, many of the "species" documented by Correvon were in fact hybrids and/or unusual selections of the species. Many of these species so labeled made it to the US and were distributed throughout the US. These did provide a wide genetic base for the work of hybridizers all over the world, as some of these selections from the wild added some unique traits to the germplasm available to hybridizers.

Two plants for which he is responsible are the velvety 'Aymon Correvon' (named for his grandson, who took over the nursery after his grandfather's death) and his namesake *heuffelii* 'Henri Correvon.' We do not know whether these plants were selections from the wild or seedlings that appeared in the nursery. 'Aymon Correvon' was formerly known as 'Correvon's Hybrid,' and it is still a wonderful plant. A medium-large rosette with a uniform silvery grey and velvety leaves tipped in dark purple. It is likely this is a hybrid of *S. wulfenii* and *S. montanum*, as it has leaf characteristics of both and a flower color that reflects yellow- and red-flowered parents. 'Henri Correvon' is a large *heuffelii* of a good clear green color with deep red-purple leaf tips. It was widely used as a parent for other hybrids.

Correvon must have had a good sense of humor as well. When a downed fence allowed sheep to enter his garden, destroying a large planting of semps, he described the sheep as "abominable razors of the globe." After deer or rabbits have nibbled on mine, I understand his exasperation but did not express it nearly as humorously.

David Ford

David Ford was one of the most prolific of the British hybridizers, and he introduced a number of really revolutionary plants, especially the cultivars of *heuffelii*. David's fascination with semps started at age twelve, beginning with the common form of *S. tectorum* in 1923 (Mentgen 1993b). David then began acquiring the hybrids of early hybridizers, such as Arends. Later, he started to breed plants himself. His first hybrid 'Hayling,' a cross of 'Commander Hay' X 'Ornatum,' was introduced in 1966. This was followed by nearly 200 other fine cultivars, about one-third being *heuffeliis*. David's cultivars also won numerous awards, including Award of Merits for 'El Toro,' 'Bella Meade,' 'State Fair,' and 'Greenstone,' and Bronze Rosettes for 'El Toro' and 'Bronze Ingot.' Although it has been thirty years since the last of David's hybrids appeared on the market, many are still available. Many of these have yet to be surpassed in their particular color range or pattern. For example, 'Bros' is still one of the most beautiful red, with almost a shocking color, and the smaller 'Mink' is just as impressive, but in much deeper and richer red colors. They are among my favorite forms of *S. heuffelii*. Perhaps David's career as a decorator (and the artist's eye) served him well in picking out the most beautiful forms of semps, too.

Fig. 8-7. David Ford (left) and Andre Smits (right).

Unlike many of us in the US, David grew all of his plants in pots. His whole small back garden was on elevated benches, with the plants arranged in pots. You can tell he had the obsession for collecting them, as they even grew on the rooftops of his shed, with a stepladder installed to observe them! Now that is an enthusiast. His collection was very well organized, with species and European and American hybrids each organized alphabetically, and with a color coordinated label that reflected the origin of a particular semp. Although he did not sell from a published list, he did have some plants for sale at the very reasonable price of 15 p ($0.50–0.75). Many came to his garden to buy these treasures, and his plants are now grown all over the world. David was a big fan of Ed Skrocki's hybridizing, and he maintained an almost complete collection of Ed's plants. The admiration was mutual, as Ed maintained a collection of all of David's hybrids, as well.

Toward the end of his life he suffered from deteriorating hearing and vision, and his collection went into decline. A neighbor's dog also contributed to the demise of his collection. David passed away in 1999, after having seventy-six years of life with semps.

Nicholas Moore

The majority of our semp hybridizers are most famous for their hybrids, but Nicholas Moore was an accomplished writer and poet, and he won several prizes for his poetry. Oddly, he was more popular with US readers than British ones, and toward the end of his life he had difficulty publishing his works. Many of the classic works of Moore have been republished, including *Spleen* (1973, a clever variety of spinoffs of a single Baudelaire poem) and *Selected Poems* (2014). He also wrote one horticultural book, *The Tall Bearded Iris* (1956), as he was also an iris enthusiast of long standing.

Nicholas's father was a professor of philosophy at Cambridge University and would take young Nicholas to the famous alpine specialist Cambria Nursery to purchase plants. From these visits Nicholas developed a love for Alpine plants and semps in particular. Again, it is amazing that a childhood experience would so influence someone for a lifetime.

Nicholas was inspired by the huge collection of David Ford and from the writings in Praegar's monograph to attempt hybridizing himself. His work was well thought out, and he quickly produced a series of hybrids, including 'Poke Eat,' 'Hey Hey,' and one of his most popular, 'Shirley's Joy,' named for his second wife in the early 1950s. 'Poke Eat' is quite an unusual name, and came about when Nicholas's children were young and were literally pokey at eating. So this is a reference to his children that he "honors" with this semp name. 'Shirley's Joy' is from a cross of *S. arachnoideum* and *S. marmoreum*, and displays many of the characteristics of both parents. After these first few sort of experimental crosses, he concentrated on just a few lines to maximize his chances for success. He had followed the breeding methods of the major bearded iris breeders in the US and knew line breeding was one of the secrets to their success, as it brought out interesting recessives and eliminated factors that muddy the results. One line involves an attempt to darken the base color of the red/green bicolor 'Commander Hay' types, resulting in the hybrid 'Corinana.' A dark red-purple line is derived from a cross of *S. tectorum* 'Nigrum' and 'S. Malby's #2' (a red, may be the same as 'Gloriosum') or similar crosses and include the cultivars 'Salacia,' 'Playcircle,' and one of my favorites, 'Akhenaten,' named for an Egyptian pharaoh. One of Moore's favorites, 'Black Claret,' combines the darker 'Commander Hay' types and the red-purple lines. Combining several of these approaches toward dark rosettes gave the lovely 'Leocadia,' 'Malarbon,' and 'Nightwood,' with the latter being especially striking. In an article in the *Sempervivum Society Journal* (Moore 1977), he describes his vision of producing better blossoms on semps so that they would complement the colors of the rosettes. He found the idea of big yellow flowers over red rosettes particularly appealing. I might agree, as even the yellow blooms of *S. heuffelii* cultivars against very red rosettes is a striking and pretty effect. A plant with the huge yellow flowers of *S. grandiflorum* with red rosette stalks would be very neat indeed.

Helen von Stein-Zeppelin

Helen von Stein-Zeppelin was a giant in the area of perennial plants, and in her nursery in Germany featured the most choice of perennials from around the world. Iris were certainly one of her specialties, and she made frequent trips to the US to attend American Iris Society conventions. The Oriental poppies that were so much a feature of the iris gardens in the US also became a fascination, and from seed from these plants Helen developed a great strain of her own. Her poppies are still considered some of the finest cultivars ever developed. She was also fascinated by semps and came to visit Bill Nixon when she was at the Boston American Iris Society convention. Helen's nursery sold a large number of cultivars and was responsible for bringing many of the US cultivars to the European market. She had a keen eye for picking out choice forms of all perennials and did much to raise the quality of the plants offered to the public. For this work in promoting and breeding so many choice perennials she was awarded the prestigious Arends Award.

Helen introduced several outstanding seedlings of her own breeding. 'Grunrand,' a large bright rosette with a thin margin of green on each leaf, is one of the most striking, but unfortunately a very slow growing cultivar. 'Maria Laach' is a most unusual plant, basically a large pale brown rosette with broad tips of nearly black. The rosettes go through several color changes over the season.

Ben Zonneveld

Ben Zonneveld is a plant scientist at the University of Leiden in the Netherlands who turned his attention to semps and later hosta. Besides his contributions in the production of new varieties, he also published a number of scholarly articles on the taxonomy of the semp species and was co-author of the most recent taxonomic status of the group. Luckily, he has also turned his interest to creating new hybrids.

In the traditional semps, I feel his greatest semp is the cultivar 'Aross,' an inspired cross of *S. arachnoideum* and *S. ossetiense*, with the name reflecting these two parents. 'Aross' has very long, narrow leaves that are strongly flushed with red. The tufts of hair at the end of each leaf almost appear like a frosting on the tips of the leaves and as a rosette as a whole. Surprisingly for such a wide cross, 'Aross' is fertile, and cross to *S. pumilum* gave the tiny maroon 'Pumaros.' A very good attempt at a blue semp is Ben's 'Blue Bird,' which has a bit of violet overlaying the blue rosette to enhance the effect.

It is the *heuffelii* and hybrids from them where the Zonneveld plants really excel. In the standard *heuffelii* cultivars, 'Orange Tip' may be the best of those currently available in the US gold *heuffelii* cultivars for growth. The color starts early, and the contrast of the very orange-red tips sets off the whole rosette. 'Vesta' has one of the prettiest pattern of any *heuffelii*, with very symmetrical rosettes that have rather dark reddish purple leaves with distinct green tips. A number of the names for his *heuffelii* cultivars are from Greek mythology, either characters or places from this age, such as 'Aphrodite,' 'Ikaros,' 'Ithaca,' and 'Paris.' Ben also created the first series of hybrids between the rollers and *heuffelii* now contained under the aggregate hybrid name *S. x nixonii* to honor Bill Nixon. My favorite of these is 'Jowan,' a red brown plant with very good growth habits, although all of them are nice plants. They have the rosette increase habit of *heuffelii*, but have a different rosette shape that reflects more of the roller parent. These plants are sterile or nearly so. I have gotten the occasional viable appearing seed, but most ovules are aborted even in stalks that have had the chance to be pollinated by a more fertile parent.

Martin Haberer

Fig. 8-8. Martin Haberer

Martin wanted to be a forester, but his eyesight made that career untenable, so he apprenticed as a gardener instead, eventually studying landscaping. For thirty years, he taught horticulture and landscaping at several institutions. His interest in semps came about after a trip to the mountains, where he saw them growing in the wild. Upon returning, he obtained a few cultivars from nurseries; these first varieties were grown on his new garage roof! Eventually, the roof was filled and large areas of the garden were filled with pots of cultivars. Perhaps because he was introduced to semps through the wild forms, these remain some of his favorites.

Although he was told to scrupulously cut off the flowering stalks to prevent the cultivars from being contaminated by seedlings, in 1974, he harvested seed from the semps growing on the roof. When the seedlings came up he was amazed at the colors and shapes of them. Most of Martin's seedlings are from known pod parents, but most of the seedlings arose from open pollination. Martin's cultivars are some of the finest available, and a number of them have made it to the US market. His hybrids cover the complete range of colors, rosette sizes, and types. Several of his greens are outstanding and very distinct plants as well: 'Reinhard,' with very dark-tipped leaves; 'Nico,' with strong red tips; 'Uranus,' a possible *S. cantabricum* hybrid with glowing green color and purple tips; and 'Bronco,' a pale green with brown tips. His reds are also justly famous. 'Fuego' is a big, brilliant rose red and it truly is *fuego* (hot!). One of my favorites and a good healthy plant. Other reds of Martin's that are also great garden plants are the red-purple with deeper center 'Irazu,' rose red thinly edged green Award of Merit winner 'Paricutin,' and classic deep red 'Max Frei,' named for the famous German horticulturalist. We are gradually importing more of his plants to the US and I look forward to seeing many more here.

Besides his work in hybridizing, Martin has been a prolific writer of gardening books in German, including one on hardy succulents and cacti (Haberer and Graf 2010). As you might imagine, semps are very well covered in this book and are illustrated with many of Martin's lovely photographs.

Andre Smits

Belgian Andre' Smits is the most prolific hybridizer of semps, literally introducing thousands of cultivars to the market. His interest in semps started in 1975, after meeting alpine specialists Roger Springael and Hugo Phillips. Further visits with Ben Zonneveld and Martin Haberer started him on the road to a full commitment to the genus. Unlike many semp enthusiasts that grow plants in pots only, Martin brought in one hundred tons of rock to create a wonderful garden, with semps as the star of the picture. The photos of his garden on the internet show just what can be done in designing with semps and just growing these plants in total excess. There are literally rivers of them!

It is nearly impossible to synthesize the work of this very prolific hybridizer, especially the 2,000 cultivars of *S. heuffelii*. Rather, I am going to describe some of his cultivars that we have available here in the US and that are sold regularly by US dealers. André named a number of plants for other hybridizers, including Ed Skrocki, Martin Haberer, and Howard Wills.

André has introduced a number of interesting variations in the cobweb and tufted groups. One of my favorites is 'Baronesse,' which is larger than most tufted/cobwebs and has a very pretty red spring color and a very strong webbing as well, even though this appears to be a hybrid, not a full cobweb. 'Koko Flanel' is a most unusual variation; the leaves are stouter than the usual cobweb and are strongly flushed with red and with an overall frosting, sort of like mini-Christmas trees. The cobwebbing is limited to the center of the rosette. 'White Ladies' is a full cobweb, and a *very* full cobweb it is. So thick that the plant really does look white.

Fig 8-9. 'Koko Flanel'

In the non-cobweb or tufted group there are several of my favorites of all semps. Three smallish rosettes that are great garden plants are 'Fromika' (sometimes sold as 'Fronika'), 'Terracotta Baby,' and 'Koressia.' All have stout rosettes that have very good garden health and make tidy clumps. 'Fromika' and 'Koressia' are more red-toned, whereas 'Terracotta Baby' has a hint of brown or tan to the color. Another smaller rosette with great color but totally different form is 'The Flintstones,' a maroon red with long, narrow, upright leaves. All of these are interesting parents too. 'Pink Minou' has just arrived in this country, but is impressive, in that you do not have to imagine the pink. Another recent arrival is 'Persephone.' This has some of the widest leaves of any cultivar and a beautiful flush of red in the spring. This may be my favorite of any cultivar that is not my own. 'Gallivarda' goes through the most changes of any cultivar that I grow, although it is always colorful. In the spring it is at its best when it is a truly glowing red. 'Yvette' shows its S. grandiflorum heredity in its bright green leaves with purple tips, but in a much nicer form and clump habit than the species. The large yellow flowers are typical of the species.

I only know two of the heuffelii types of Andrés, but they are both nice. 'Applauze' is red with a green edge to the leaves, but it is most interesting in winter, when it gets almost black in color. The seedlings from this cultivar are most interesting too, giving several unusual shades of olive green, purple, and red. 'Clown' is just fun—basically a green rosette with splashes and stripes of red on the green background. In Oregon I see less of the splashing, but the form is also unique, with very broad leaves and quite a large rosette. Totally cool. This is one where I am very excited about my first crop of seedlings from open pollination.

Volkmar Schara

Fig. 8-10. Volkmar Schara and his son Leopold.

Volkmar Schara is one of the newer stars on the semp scene, but he is making himself well known for his many outstanding hybrids. Not all of these have reached the US, but those that have are getting rave reviews here, too. Although it appears most of Volkmar's selections are from open pollinated seed, he does keep the records of the seed parent so that information is known. Volkmar has created a number of very unique cobwebbed and tufted types, which is no easy feat. Of those now in the US, there are bright red tufted 'Lucy Liu,' a very webbed, almost bubbly in appearance cobwebbed 'Shampoo,' and the neat, heavily tufted, near cobweb 'Nelda.' Volkmar used my

'Flasher' to create the orange-toned and very bright 'Orange Glow,' which is fast becoming one of the most popular new plants here in the US. Other bright-colored semps from Volkmar include the almost maroon centered 'Tesoro,' large and bright red 'Jumimond,' and yellow-orange 'Saffarasome.' One of his most popular cultivars in Europe is the very dark and wide-leaved 'Leopold,' which is named for his son. Plants of this cultivar have finally reached the US. I am excited about seeing the remainder of his plants in the US.

◄ Fig. 8-11. 'Leopold'

➤ Fig. 8-12. 'Orange Glow'

Volkmar Schara was unknown to me when I started growing semps again in my new Oregon home. A visit to Edelweiss Nursery in Canby, Oregon, and I walked out of there with a semp named 'Killer' that would change my breeding program. Luckily, a plant of this cultivar was blooming and that flower was carefully self-pollinated to start my breeding program again. In addition, the blooms the next year, when crossed with my 'Jungle Shadows,' gave an incredible spread of seedlings. Thank you Volkmar for rekindling my program, as well as having a great one of your own.

Erwin Geiger

Fig. 8-13. Erwin Geiger

Erwin is the youngest of the hybridizers described in this book, and he has already made a big impact on the semp world. We have been email pen pals since I moved to Oregon, as he had many questions about the early US hybrids and their origins, and I wanted to know what was happening on the German scene. Like many of us, he developed an early fascination with these plants. His grandmother presented him with his first semps, growing in a planter. An order from Helen von Stein-Zeppelin's nursery sealed the deal. He was totally fascinated by these plants and has not looked back. After interning in a prominent German nursery, Erwin has established his own nursery that is devoted to semps and other hardy succulents. Each year he offers a selection of plants from his own breeding, plus a number of choice and unusual varieties from around the world. This is like a candy shop for semp enthusiasts, and I admit to having shopped there. I only wish it were easier to get plants from the EU into the US!

Erwin started by growing seed from Thompson and Morgan (most likely from Ed Skrocki's large collection), and from this seedling crop he named 'Cornflake Girl,' 'Crucify,' and 'Hugo.' Erwin is a big Tori Amos fan, and has named several cultivars for her songs. Erwin has let bees do most of his crossing, choosing to raise seedlings from cultivars in which he has interest.

Erwin must have some very talented bees, as he has produced a number of wonderful cultivars! 'Goldmarie,' a bright, almost orange cultivar at times that can get quite large, has grown very well in the Pacific Northwest, and is also an excellent increaser. This is going to

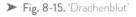

Fig. 8-14. Erwin Geiger nursery

➤ Fig. 8-15. 'Drachenblut'

be a classic semp. From open-pollinated seed of David Ford's great 'Red Shadows,' Erwin hit the jackpot with a wonderful group of dark red to red-purples, including 'Drachenblut' (translates to 'Dragon's Blood'), 'Dornroschen' (translates to 'Sleeping Beauty'), 'Diavolo,' the much paler 'Rita Rose,' and the strong red-green bicolor 'Lemon Kiss.' Very good work, bees! Erwin's hybridizing has extended into all shapes and sizes, from the large red-green bicolor 'Picasso' to the tiny 'Regensberg Knirps,' a seedling of the small 'Little Mary Sunshine' and with thicker leaves like the Skrocki classic 'Plastic.' Most recently, Erwin has turned his talents to the *heuffelii* cultivars, introducing the clear raspberry rose 'Raspberry Swirl,' dark red-purple with lighter edge 'Thor,' and the dark smaller one 'Kleiner Krieger.' We have recently imported a number of Erwin's cultivars to the US, and there are some very exciting things coming from this hybridizer. With his good eye for finding new cultivars and his youth, I expect great things from his work.

Erwin and I share the goal of creating a totally black semp, and he has a seedling that at least fleetingly has this color. Stay tuned, I am sure he will eventually select for year-round black color.

Howard Wills

Fig. 8-16. Howard Wills with the author, inspecting the author's seedlings.

Howard's interest in semps started as for many of us, in his youth. A great aunt maintained a collection of succulents in pots. In one of these pots was *S. arachnoideum*, described by her as the "cobweb cactus." This intrigued the young Wills, and a gift of this plant sealed the deal. As he describes, "From then on I was hooked" (Wills 2004). His hobby spilled over into establishing a nursery.

Howard runs Fernwood Nursery in the UK, offering an outstanding collection of semp species and hybrids in their annual lists. We were lucky in the US to get some of the last imports from this nursery, so many of the plants of Howard's own breeding and other fine plants from the UK have made it to the US. At Fernwood, the plants are grown mainly in pots and the pots are displayed on staging made out of concrete structures that allow for easy observation of the plants. Construction of the staging is described more fully in the culture section of this book. Besides their interest in semps, Fernwood also maintains a collection of *Phormium*.

Howard has written three short books on semps that are a great resource for semp enthusiasts, the most recent being *An Introduction to Sempervivum and Jovibarba Species and Cultivars* (2004). This book has many excellent photographs taken by the author and the text provides an introduction to the group. Two earlier versions of this book are also valuable, as they contain slightly different viewpoints and more extensive cultivar lists. These books served as an inspiration for this much larger book.

Howard was a friend of prolific hybridizer David Ford and still lists many of his cultivars in his price list. Howard also began hybridizing semps himself and has produced a number of outstanding hybrids. Some of my favorites are the green with bright red tips 'Fernwood,' large red with green tips 'Starburst,' spikey red 'Marland Ruby,' unusual red-purple 'Squib,' velvety green near cobweb 'Green Ice,' and the unusual large brown-grey blend 'Lion King,' one of my favorites of all the semps. Although not a hybrid, Howard introduced the *S. calcareum* 'Extra' that has the most amazingly symmetrical arrangement of leaves that enhances the pattern of purple tips on the green leaves. It is my favorite *S. calcareum* cultivar. The intense and smallish *heuffelii* 'Be Mine' is one of my favorites of Howard's plants—a very neat plant. All of Howard's plants are good growers and very distinct, as one might expect from one with an extensive collection.

Sue Thomas

English hybridizer Sue Thomas has hit the hybridizing scene in a big way, producing a large number of hybrids. Unlike other hybridizers, her plants are sold through a wholesale nursery, Sunray Plants in Haccombe/Devon, England. Close to three hundred plants have been named, and many of the names use three "stable names." 'Devon,' 'Haccombe,' and 'Sunray' are names associated with the location or the nursery. Unfortunately, most of these hybrids have not made it to the US, but those that have are being well received. 'Purple Dazzler' is a very showy, large plant with bright purple leaf bases and green tips. This plant is a good grower and very healthy. 'Frothy Coffee' is a medium-sized rosette with red-brown color (must be a latte!) with the velvety leaves giving a sort of frosted appearance. 'Sunray Magic' is a large plant with strong red leaf bases and green tops to each leaf. The shape is similar to 'Purple Dazzler,' indicating they might be related. Her two fine roller introductions, 'Limette' and 'Alpine Fire,' are great advances in this group of semps. 'Devil's Touch' is one of the hottest semps on the scene in the US, an unusual brown with darker tips and long, spidery leaves. We hope that more of her hybrids reach the US soon, as there are a number that appear very intriguing.

AMERICAN NURSERY PEOPLE

Sandy MacPherson

Sandy MacPherson ran MacPherson's Garden in Oregon, Ohio, from 1947 until the late seventies; it was the primary source for everyone in the US to obtain their plants during this period. His list of plants was a one-page affair with the same price for each plant (.75 cents in 1964) with no descriptions, just a list of names. When you ordered from him you received a *clump*. Not surprisingly, with quality and price like that, he did well selling semps. He was the main source for Helen Payne's and Polly Bishop's large collections.

Sandy had purchased all of the stock plants from Sanford's Nursery, as well as plants from Carl Purdy. In addition to his catalog, Sandy produced a little informational brochure with photographs and a brief description of the species and basic culture information. For many years, that was our only real modern "publication" to which we could refer. The color pictures were a good advertisement, so despite the lack of descriptions in his list, the pictures sold lots of plants.

Besides selling plants that were produced by others, Sandy discovered a number of fine cultivars that arose from open pollinated seed falling among the stock plants. These plants formed an outstanding group of plants. These hybrids include: 'Laura Lee,' named for his granddaughter, a rosy red with prominent hairy tufts on each leaf, 'Mauvine,' a blue green with a touch of rose on the edge and tips of leaves; 'Silverine,' the first real silver-colored rosette and of large size, an outstanding parent; 'Clara Noyes,' a small velvety orange red with very good health; and 'Rita Jane,' a dark olive with very broad leaves and a small purple tip. Perhaps Sandy's biggest contribution to the semp world was the discovery of the sport known as 'Oddity' growing among the plant then known as 'Albidum' (a *tectorum* type). And *odd* it is. This is what Helen Payne termed "quilled" and is an apt description, as the leaves are rolled back on to themselves and form a hollow tube that resembles the quills on a porcupine's back. 'Rita Jane' and 'Oddity' won Bronze Rosettes from the Sempervivum Society and are very deserving winners. Both were in my garden in Massachusetts as a kid and they are still in my garden in Oregon.

Helen Payne

Helen Payne has often been described as the matriarch of the American *Sempervivum* movement. She certainly took the US scene to new heights. Helen's interest in semps started in the late 1950s, and continued until she was no longer able to stay at home. Like many of that era, Helen's interest started with an order of plants from Sandy MacPherson. After seeing the plants she was hooked, and it began her lifelong love affair with these plants.

Helen, with her husband Slim (R. N.) Payne, ran her Oakhill Gardens in Dallas, Oregon, a small community near Salem, Oregon. Unlike others before her, Helen published a catalog with a huge number of cultivars, each with good (and tempting) descriptions of the offerings in the catalog. Besides the good descriptions, Helen introduced to the world the hybrids of Ed Skrocki, Pat Drown, Gary Gossett, Mina Colvin, C. William Nixon, and Kevin Vaughn, as well as a few of her own. Helen was a master of organization. The beds of cultivars were very carefully separated so that only the correct plants would be sent, and she personally packed each box to ensure that only the correct ones were sent. The plants were shipped very carefully in paper bags clearly labeled, and one always received at least one large mother rosette with several increase. This ensured many repeat customers. In addition, her collection of sedums was second to none, so people would often try a few semps in an order of sedums and suddenly become addicted to the charms of semps too. It is not surprising that with good marketing, good product, and huge variety, Helen was very successful, despite the now outrageously low price of $1.25 for a new introduction!

Helen's own introductions show you something of her frugal nature. Sandy MacPherson was less scrupulous than others in removing bloomstalks, so besides the cultivar that you ordered frequently small seedlings would also come in the package. When these arrived in Helen's nursery she cleaned these imposter plants out, but instead of disposing of them, she rowed out the seedlings so they could be evaluated. Helen had a good eye for something new and interesting, so she picked out such classics as 'Lavender and Old Lace,' 'Carmen,' and 'Elene' from these plants that would have otherwise been castoffs. 'Lavender and Old Lace' was awarded a Gold Rosette by the Sempervivum Society. She also renamed a few other cultivars with less-than-great commercial names. Gary Gossett named a plant in her honor, although it is fairly well hidden. In his 'Pacific Hep,' the Hep part of the name stands for Helen E. Payne, and is even more of a disguise than when Helen named 'Elene' for herself. A sedum cultivar, probably a *Sedum spathulifolium* selection, was also named for Helen. In 2015, the semp I named 'Helen Payne' came on the market and it is a seedling of my 'Jungle Shadows' that she admired so many years ago.

Perhaps Helen's biggest contribution to the world of semps is her book *Plant Jewels of the High Country, Sempervivums and Sedums*, published in 1972 by Pine Cone publishers in Medford, Oregon. At last we had a book filled with color photographs. It soon became a classic for semp enthusiasts in the US, although there were numerous errors in taxonomy. These were mostly not Helen's fault, but rather, she described the plants as they were passed on to her by other nursery people. In fact, she saved these designations religiously until the correct type plants were received from Peter Mitchell. In her book, she mentions two very youthful hybridizers—Gary Gossett and Kevin Vaughn—who would go on

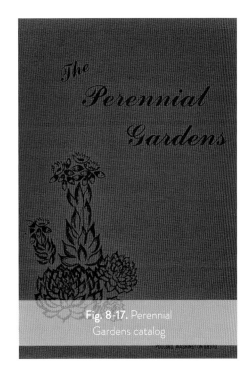

Fig. 8-17. Perennial Gardens catalog

to create many hybrids. It was good that Helen had faith in us! For me, the most interesting part of her book was not so much the material on the semps, but rather, her stories of finding interesting selections of sedum in the wild, as well as her unabashed enthusiasm for using these plants in unusual ways. Although this book is long out of print, it can frequently be found through internet book sellers and is a nice addition to your library.

Helen sold off the mail order portion of her nursery to Shirley Rempel (Alpine Gardens), which was subsequently sold to Dick Cavender to become Red's Rhodies and Alpine Gardens, so the plants from her nursery were all preserved by others. Helen continued to sell plants at her home and at farmer's markets until she was forced to quit because of ill health.

Betty Bronow (The Perennial Garden)

Betty Bronow gardened in Poulsbo, Washington, and like many that eventually establish a nursery, it was her love of the plants that took her on the path to selling plants. Hers was the first multi-page booklet as a catalog, and with much more expansive descriptions of the plants, as well. She imported many plants from Europe, and was also responsible for introducing the cultivars of Ed Skrocki and Polly Bishop, as well as her own hybridizing. Betty was also a frequent contributor to the *Sempervivum Fanciers Association Newsletter* and the *Journal of the Sempervivum Society*, with articles on culture or her opinions on the new cultivars. Everyone who has ever known Betty has commented as to "what a nice person she was." What a great way to be remembered, something to which we may all aspire.

With all these new cultivars at her disposal, it was not surprising that she would try her hand at hybridizing. She produced a very nice series of hybrids in just a few years of hybridizing. She was a big fan of Tolkein's *Lord of the Rings*, and she named a series of her hybrids from characters of the book: 'Faramir,' 'Legolas,' 'Meriadoc,' 'Theoden,' 'Frodo,' 'Treebeard,' 'Boromir,' 'Eomer,' 'Eowyn,' 'Fredegar,' and 'Gollum.' This was very clever marketing, and moreover, the plants themselves are quite choice, too. Somehow these plants seem to look more like their namesakes as well, with darker characters like 'Gollum' being an appropriately different-appearing semp. Several of these come from a most interesting cross of 'Bronze Pastel' X 'Jungle Fires,' which combines a lot of different genetic material, and you can see the effects of both parents and grandparents of these plants in the progeny.

Her 'Pippin' won a Gold Rosette from the Sempervivum Society and is still a lovely cultivar. 'Strider,' a seedling from 'Atropurpureum' with exceptionally long and narrow red-purple leaves, has always been one of my favorites, as has the uniquely-formed and frequently crested 'Butterbur.'

Besides the award for 'Pippin,' Betty was awarded the Hybridizer Award from the Washington State Federation of Garden Clubs for her work with semps. The only semp hybridizer so honored, to my knowledge.

Betty suffered from ill health and she was only able to maintain her mail order business for a few years. Her last plants, including many of the *Lord of the Rings* series, were introduced by Squaw Mountain Gardens.

Squaw Mountain Gardens and SMG Succulents

Like many things, this nursery started off quite by accident. Joyce and John Hoekstra were out driving around the countryside and came upon a sign for Oakhill Gardens. After seeing the semps Joyce was hooked. This was the first of many visits and purchases. Joyce became friendly with Helen, and Slim and John were kindred souls, too. After several years of purchases, Helen suggested that Joyce might get into the nursery business and showed Joyce some of the techniques that she used to propagate and ship plants. The "hobby

◄ **Fig. 8-18.** Joyce Hoekstra

➤ **Fig. 8-19.** Cobwebs at Squaw Mountain Gardens.

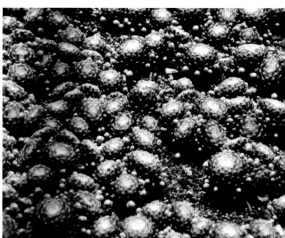

nursery" started in 1983, with a small sheltered alpine house that John constructed for Joyce. Several years later, Dick Cavender, who had taken over the Alpine Gardens franchise from Shirley Rempel, was looking to concentrate his efforts solely on rhododendrons and sold that part of the business to the Hoekstras. This purchase greatly increased the number of varieties that were offered, essentially providing all of the cultivars that Oakhill Gardens had once owned. Squaw Mountain Gardens sat on a seven acre piece of property in the foothills of beautiful Mount Hood. This proved to be an ideal place to grow over 1,000 varieties of semps and sedums. With approximately 13,000 square feet of covered alpine houses, the plants were protected and grown perfectly. Clearly semp growers have never had it so good for both plant quality and variety.

Janis Noyes, Joyce's daughter, became interested in semps and began to help her parents in the nursery, and not long after her husband Art became part of the operation and eventually they became full owners. Besides the mail order business, Squaw Mountain was a vendor for the Fred Meyer stores on the West Coast, producing displays that showed how the plants could be planted, as well as a diverse collection of semps and sedums in pots. This was a great way to introduce general gardeners to the joys of semps. It was also serendipitous, in that semp hybridizer Gary Gossett was the person in charge of the Fred Meyers operation at the time; a great relationship developed between Squaw Mountain Gardens and the hybridizer. A majority of Gary's Pacific series were introduced by Squaw Mountain. Janis also introduced her own cultivar 'Dreamcaster,' a nice red tufted type. The last hybrids of Betty Bronow were also introduced in the Squaw Mountain Gardens catalog, including several of the *Lord of the Rings* series.

Unfortunately gardeners do wear out! After over twenty years in business, Janis and Art were looking to retire and do something different with their lives. Amazingly enough, Don Mylin happened by one day just as Janis and Art were thinking about tapering down and inquired as to whether the business was for sale. Janis and Art decided to take an entirely new path in their lives after selling the nursery and toured the country, seeing much of it before coming back to Oregon to settle into retirement. They are still growing semps, but not for sale.

Don Mylin took Squaw Mountain Gardens and renamed it SMG Succulents, as he also moved the nursery to his property and it was not really on Squaw Mountain anymore. This also proved to be advantageous, as the "succulents" in the name would allow internet searches for hardy succulents to quickly locate the nursery. Don's vision of the nursery is a bit different in that he sells retail only. His website contains hundreds of choice specimens, each illustrated with a color image and details of the size and other vital information of the plant. A simple click and you have purchased a semp. I wonder what Helen Payne and Sandy MacPherson would think of this revolution in marketing. Don's plants are grown in pots in long hoop houses, but the semps are shipped bare root, as are most in the industry.

Fig. 8-20. Don Mylin

With all these semps at his disposal, it was only natural Don might try his hand at growing seed and also selecting sports from the existing cultivars. Don confesses to using the "Skrocki method" of growing open pollinated seed for his seed, but he has done quite well with this method. 'Gingerbread Boy,' a brown-toned large rosette with dark purple tips; 'Round Midnight,' a dark medium-sized red; deep purple 'Cloud Cap' and dark red 'Midnight Sun'; and blended pastel shades 'Salt Peanuts' are some of the outstanding cultivars that have been developed. My favorite cobweb is the new 'Poco Loco,' a plant with rosettes irregularly splashed red, much like the kernels in Indian corn. 'New Rhumba' is a most interesting variegated sport; the edge is very narrow but white, and the remainder of the leaf is red, making a very neat trimmed effect. It is not a rapid increaser, but better than many other variegated plants. 'Brillante,' the variegated sport of 'Rocknoll Rosette,' is on everyone's *must have* list.

Mountain Crest Gardens

Thomas Jopson and son Matts run Mountain Crest Gardens, one of the major retail nurseries of semps in the US, selling millions of plants each year. As for many such ventures, the nursery became a semp nursery through a series of events, and no one would have predicted the subsequent course of events. Thomas started the nursery in 1995, with a primary focus of selling planters, as well as a variety of succulents, so that the home gardener could create interesting planters that were almost no fail. This portion of the nursery still exists, and they sell a very interesting and eclectic set of planters that really showcase semps well. A turn in the nursery started when the stock plants of Irene Russ, a major grower of semps in California and one of the early members of the Sempervivum Fancier's Association, was bought due to the interest of one of the nursery workers. This purchase added lots of choice cultivars to the collection that were all properly named. Today, their nursery offers over 250 different semps and 700 different succulents in total. Besides named cultivars,

Fig. 8-21. Greenhouses at Mountain Crest Gardens.

they also distribute landscape and pot garden collections of unnamed cultivars for those wanting semps but not particular varieties. Since 2014, Matts has taken over the succulent end of the business and has expanded the types of offerings. His internet and business savvy has greatly increased interest in the offerings and keeps their twenty employees busy filling orders and maintaining the stock. Although the staff at Mountain Crest do not hybridize themselves, they have introduced 'Pinkerine,' a sport of 'Silverine' found in their collection. It is a pinker version of 'Silverine.'

With their business expanding so much, they have recently purchased more property in Oregon, as the climate is so amenable to growing semps.

Chris Hansen and Chick Charms®

Chris Hansen is a man with boundless enthusiasm and energy with a horticultural pedigree at Wayside Gardens and Terra Nova Nurseries before entering his present venture. Chick Charms® is a very clever way in which semps are marketed. Chris sells Chick Charms® as wholesale items, so they are available to gardeners through a number of garden centers and other retail outlets. Each of these semps are named varieties that Chris has selected as being especially good in all aspects: rosette color, size, retention of color, and plant health. The rosettes are sold as individuals in four inch pots. Each is marked with the cute Chick Charms® logo with directions for planting and garden use on each label. The healthy plants and easy care instructions almost ensure success.

Chris has been hybridizing sedums for some time, and has produced a series of plants that have great garden value, with very attractive foliage and flowers. 'Dazzleberry' and 'Lime Twister' are two of my favorites, and both are wonderful companion plants for semps and very useful in both the rock garden and perennial borders. Chris also found a wonderful sport of 'Ruby Heart' and named it 'Gold Nugget.' Unlike most yellow semps, 'Gold Nugget' is a strong grower and a very healthy plant. We predict great things for this plant.

THREE OREGON NURSERIES:
Perennial Obsession, Young's Garden Center, and Little Prince of Oregon

In Oregon we have several boutique nurseries that sell named cultivars of semps all around the US.

Dave Jarrell and Cynda Foster run Perennial Obsessions in a scenic location just north of Salem. Cynda's interest in gardening started with her mother. Her mother bought plants from the legendary Helen Payne and Cynda caught the bug. The hobby soon became a business with husband Dave. In their nursery, plants are grown in pots and are grown under cover so that plants may be obtained most of the year. Cynda and Dave have imported a number of new European hybrids, as well as obtained semps from a large collection of a retired dealer. Thus, they have many plants that are not sold by other dealers in the US. Cynda and I met by chance at a Salem Hardy Plant Society meeting and after she expressed her interest in semps I said, "Well, I'm the one who made 'Jungle Shadows' and 'Lipstick.'" I think she was a little surprised that I was not dead at first, but I assured her I was indeed that person after I told her of my interaction with Helen Payne! She quickly spread the word to local semp enthusiast Lynn Smith, and we have regular visits to do semp talk. So nice to have semp enthusiasts in such close proximity! Cynda is an artist at making wreaths and arranging potted succulents including sedums and semps.

Toby Landers runs the semp end of the business of Young's Garden Center in Roseberg,

Oregon. Toby's dad was an accountant, and when the Young's Garden Center went up for sale he bought the company. The garden center is now a family business. Toby developed an interest in semps and developed a website to sell rosettes that was separate from the on site sales portion of the remainder of the nursery. After a visit to my garden and attendance at the clinic he started marketing some of my hybrids and has a collection of my older hybrids for sale, as well. I am sure Helen Payne would faint at the prices these new ones cost! They are no longer .75 cents Helen!

Little Prince of Oregon differs from the other two Oregon nurseries in that it is a wholesale operation, and it makes no direct sales to the public. The owners generously invited Lynn Smith and I to see their operation and the quality of the plants was amazingly impressive. In fact, some of the cultivars, such as 'Rubikon' and 'Lavender and Old Lace,' are growing so well and look better than I have ever seen them grown. All of their plants are grown in long, unheated hoop houses and are shipped in small pots. Most of these plants end up in garden centers. We are lucky to have such a great source of quality plants in the US.

Besides these three nurseries, I have already mentioned Emma Elliott's and Truls Jensen's nursery in the section on hybridizers. We are very lucky to have such great nurseries here in Oregon.

As I finish this chapter, I realize how many instances of single events changing lives of people, and also some of the legacy of our dealer members as plants from one nursery are transferred to another. Unlike many other plant groups, we have a wonderful legacy of maintaining plants so that plants from all ages are preserved and correctly named.

TWO SOCIETY FOUNDERS

Peter Mitchell

Peter Mitchell saw the need for a group on *Sempervivum*, and in 1970, he established the Sempervivum Society in England. Shortly thereafter announcements in *Flower and Garden* and the *Avant Gardener* by Kevin Vaughn solicited for people interested in the Sempervivum Society; these names and addresses were forwarded to Peter so that the group had a good US representation. For over twenty years Peter produced the *Sempervivum Society Journal* that included discussions of taxonomy, including new species and descriptions of some of the better hybrids. Peter maintained a reference collection and sold plants of these to members so that verified plants were available for all of the members. The history of this collection is impressive. Praegar's original plants as described in his monograph were passed on to alpine and iris specialist Hugh Miller, and these were transferred to Alan Smith in 1957. These served as the basis of the Mitchell collection. Accessions from the collecting trips in Spain of Dr. Mark Smith and of Turkey from a number of botanists were added to this collection for newly described species. Thus, the collection of very carefully documented specimens, verified by leading taxonomists, served as the basis of this collection. At last, the very confusing taxonomy of these plants was on much firmer footing.

Fig. 8-22. *Sempervivum* Society logo

In addition, two different competitions were set up to award worthy cultivars. One, on unintroduced plants, led to an Award of Merit. The other, for plants already on the market, led to three levels of rosette award: gold, silver, and bronze. (Most of the winners of these competitions are noted either in the cultivar list or with the hybridizer that won these awards.) Moreover, because the plants in these competitions were obtained from the hybridizer, their identity was also ensured.

Peter was much more interested in species than in cultivars, and even expressed his view of hybridizers as "mere raisers of seed." He did have a point, in that many cultivars being introduced were too similar to older cultivars or had growth or health issues. Nonetheless, his wife Mary did produce some hybrids from hand-pollinated seed and from this the hybrids 'Highland Mist' and 'Cabaret' were introduced. Both Peter and Mary are credited with the creation of these plants.

The Sempervivum Society was given the registration authority for the genus and Peter prepared the one (and only, as far as I know) checklist of plants named through 1982, published in 1985. This list established the precedence of all these names to this point and was a great service to the group. When the Sempervivum Society ceased existence in the 1990s, there was no society to keep track of new names, nor to enforce the rules for naming new plants. Several groups have attempted to fill this void by publishing annotated lists of plants and obtaining photographs of the genuine plants so that there is some semblance of order in the naming of new plants, and that at least authenticated photos can be compared with a plant in question. (These sites are described in the appendix.)

Besides his work for the society, Peter also produced a book that is of use to semp enthusiasts. *The Sempervivum and Jovibarba Handbook* (1973) is mostly a botanical treatise of the species, as there was so much confusion at the time the book was written. Only a handful of hybrids are described toward the end of the book, although, as the author notes, in 1973, there was not the variety of hybrids available in the UK as there was in the US. Since that time the number and quality of hybrids has greatly increased.

Bill Nixon

Bill Nixon is actually Dr. C. William Nixon, a professor of genetics for many years at Simmons College in Boston. His professional work was on the coat color genetics of hamsters, although he had also worked with the house plant *Sinningia*, developing some quite nice miniature cultivars. A mutual acquaintance of Bill and I had been in Polly Bishop's and my garden during an iris tour in 1969, and admired the variety of semps. When Bill and this acquaintance were talking gardening my name came up and he mentioned that, "This kid Kevin is breeding them." A quick phone call and he was off to visit Polly Bishop and me. He left with pieces of virtually everything we owned, which was most of the cultivars and species then available in the US, plus some of our seedlings. He was hopelessly hooked after that and made semps his single devotion afterward. Bill became a member of the round robin letter that I was then circulating between the semp enthusiasts in the US. This would arrive about twice each year, filled with information and photos from the members. Although this kept the US group together, it was *very* slow (think of snail mail going to eight different people before you see it!), and there was no way to get information out to everybody, or to increase the size beyond this small group. Bill sent out a first issue of the *Sempervivum Fancier's Association*

Fig. 8-23. Masthead for the *Sempervivum Fancier's Association Newsletter.*

Newsletter (SFAN) with members of the round robin as founding members of the group. We had a group in the US! Bill took photos and then inserted the photos into the spots on mimeographed pages. He assembled and often wrote a majority of these issues. As with the Sempervivum Society, after Bill stopped producing SFAN there was no longer a group. Bill would have been very difficult to replace, as he possessed the knowledge and writing skills to pull off this endeavor. For a while there was a publication called *SempWorld* published by Glenn Mentgen, but it too soon faded. A broader group, the Winter Hardy Cactus and Succulent Association, operated for a few years and published some great publications, but it too ceased operation.

Besides Bill's role in the formation of SFA, he produced many outstanding hybrids, especially in the *S. heuffelii* group, which became his favorites. Toward the end of his gardening they were the only plants left. (Many of these are described in the cultivar section of this book.) The red cultivars 'Inferno,' 'Hot Lips,' 'Geronimo,' 'Mystique,' and 'Torrid Zone' are among my favorites, although Bill favored 'Nannette,' which was named for his mother. Two green cultivars, 'Sundancer' and 'Sunny Side Up,' are probably seedlings of 'Pallasii,' and are improvements on this classic form. The red cultivars especially set a high standard for *S. heuffelii* types and served as the breeding material for other hybridizers. All have proven to be useful parents. Other semps of merit from Bill's hybridizing include the large watermarked green 'Jolly Green Giant,' the very blue-toned 'Twilight Blues,' and the small but intense purple 'Purple Passion.' Bill also named the cultivar of unknown origin 'Canada Kate,' a semp with an unusual shade of pastel green rosette.

The Dalton Project: Bill Nixon and Winnie Crane

Another huge contribution of Bill's was to straighten out the very confusing nomenclature that existed in the US at that time. Often times the same plant would be sold under different names, or conversely, different plants would be sold under the same name. This was very frustrating for gardeners who wished to have the correct names on their plants, and equally frustrating for nursery owners who wanted to sell the correct plants.

Fig. 8-24. Winnie Crane

Winnie Crane operated Sugar Hill Nursery in Dalton, Massachusetts, where she sold geraniums (she would always remind me "Geraniums are crane's bills"), fuschias, and of course, semps. Her ivy leaf geranium (*Pelargonium*) 'Sugar Baby' was a revolution, and even after sixty years since its introduction, it is still the most widely grown ivy leaf geranium. The semps were used in most interesting ways. Carlton Deame, Mrs. Crane's head gardener, would take large pieces of driftwood and have holes drilled in them to accommodate colonies of semps. The holes were filled with Milorganite and single plants or small colonies were planted in each crevice. In several seasons the semps would fill in the cavity and spill beyond it, creating living sculptures. These were displayed as sculptures on a gravel or concrete base, and were truly works of art. In addition, she had a large planting of individually named cultivars. Her unique display inspired many to try semps in their gardens.

Winnie decided to help straighten out the names of the cultivars and species, as often times a plant from one nursery would not match the offerings from another despite the same name. To address this, all of the nurseries in the US contributed samples of the cultivars and Mrs. Crane bought the reference specimens from Peter Mitchell. All together there were more than 300 cultivars investigated. These were grown in an area about the size of a football field, planted in identical potting mix. Each cultivar was grown in a block, with all the plants from each nursery, plus the reference plant, grown in a separate area within the block so that specimens from each source could be examined under essentially identical conditions. Each of these plants were examined by a panel consisting of Bruce and Wilhemina Neil, Bill Nixon, and Winnie over the course of several years. Perhaps mistakenly, no plant was allowed to flower, for fear that seeds would contaminate the entries. This did eliminate the chance for stray contaminating seedlings, but also eliminated bloom color and other characteristics that might have been useful in discriminating similar but not identical cultivars. Out of the 300 cultivars, more than 200 were verified as correct, although a large number could not be positively identified. Each nursery that contributed plants to the study were given samples of the correct plant to grow on, so that at least in 1975, the nurseries in the US were growing mostly correctly identified plants. I can't imagine trying a similar thing today with 7,000 cultivars and species accessions to examine.

Winnie was a tour de force in all aspects of her life and never did just a little. She won numerous awards at the prestigious New York and Boston Flower shows for her exhibits and she was awarded the Natalie Peters Medal from the Garden Clubs of America for finding unusual plant material and using it creatively. Certainly her living sculptures that she created with semps in driftwood qualified her for this honor. Besides her horticultural interests, she was an accomplished pianist and was behind the development of the Boston Symphony's summer home in the Berkshire Mountains of Massachusetts that eventually became the famed Tanglewood summer music festival. We are lucky that Winnie was interested in *Sempervivum* and had no fear about tackling such an ambitious project.

PRESENT DAY ORGANIZATIONS/GROUPS

Since then, the Germans have taken the lead in the world of organizations: they publish a magazine called *SemperPost* and have meetings of enthusiasts of breeders. Unfortunately for those with English as a primary (or only!) language, the magazine is only useful for the photos. The Germans also have a gathering of enthusiasts that allows for purchase of plants and comparison of new hybrids, as well as just good camaraderie. In the US, a group of enthusiasts is served by the internet chat group National Gardening Association that is moderated by Lynn Smith and Chris Rentmeister. Within the *Sempervivum* group, a site has been set up to include photos and descriptions of the cultivars that are being grown to eliminate incorrectly identified plants. Members may ask and answer questions, post pictures, or call attention to new plants and/or group activities. This group served as the nucleus for the hybridizer's clinic that we host in Salem, Oregon, that has a growing group of enthusiastic attendees.

REFERENCES

Bloom A (1991) *Alan Bloom's Hardy Perennials. New Plants Raised and Introduced by a Lifelong Plantsman*. Batsford Ltd. London

Gossett G (1985) "Questions and answers." *Sempervivum Fanciers Association Newsletter* 11: 12

Haberer M, Graf H (2010) *500 Winterharte Sukkulenten & Kakteen*. Ulmer Eugen Verlag, Germany

Mentgen G (1993a) "Titans in the world of semps: Ed Skrocki." *SempWorld* Winter 1992–1993: 8–9

Mentgen G (1993b) "People behind the plants: David Ford." *SempWorld* Spring 1993: 7–9

Mitchell P (1973) *The Sempervivum and Jovibarba Handbook*. The Sempervivum Society. Burgess Hill, Sussex, England.

Moore, N (1977) "Enduring beauty, on the purpose of hybridizing." *Sempervivum Society Journal* 8(1):16-19

Payne HE (1972) *Plant Jewels of the High Country*. Pine Cone Publishers. Medford, OR

Peckham EAS (1940) *American Iris Society Alphabetical Iris Check List*. Waverly Press. Baltimore, MD

Purdy C (1976) *My Life and My Times*. Naturegraph Press. Happy Camp, CA

Shinn CH, Burbank L, Purdy C (1901) "Intensive Horticulture in California." Reprints from *Land of Sunshine* magazine

Wills H, Wills S (2004) *An Introduction to* Sempervivum *and Jovibarba*. Fernwood Nursery, UK

A N N O T A T E D
B I B L I O G R A P H Y , W E B S I T E S ,
A N D   S O U R C E S

BOOKS

Although there have been few books that feature *Sempervivum*, there are a few that should be part of a semp enthusiast's library. Most of these are long out of print, but may be obtained from used book dealers and on the internet:

Praeger, L (1932) *An Account of the Sempervivum Group.*
Royal Horticultural Society, London.

This is really a reference work with descriptions of species. Praeger's was the first serious attempt to describe the species, and it is a fine attempt, as he was able to discern the species from the hybrids, ending much of the confusion up to that point. Many of his taxonomic decisions stand to this day. Also included in this work are the "tropical relatives" of semps from the Canary Islands, such as Aeonium and Monathes, which we now know are only morphologically similar, not closely related. Although the original book is long out of print, there was a reprint of the work in 1967 that I own and a more modern reprint that is easily available. Although many taxonomic sources are dull, Praeger's writing style makes these even relatively dull details much more exciting.

Payne, HE (1972) *Plant Jewels of the High Country.*
Pine Cone Publishers. Medford, Oregon

At the time Helen wrote this book, her Oakhill Gardens in Dallas, Oregon, was one of the premier nurseries for semps and sedums in the US. The book tells the story of her nursery and shows many pictures of how the plants are grown, both in display beds and in more artistic sorts of arrangements. The photos are of variable quality and the nomenclature represents the state of confusion here in the US nursery trade at this time. To me, the most interesting portions of this book are her stories of tracking down wild sedums and finding the rare hybrids of species.

Correvon, H (1932) *Les Joubarbes,*
English Translation, the Sempervivum Society

I am lucky to have received an English translation of this work that was published by the Sempervivum Society, although I have read some of the original publication in French. The translation is very good. The French version is available as a free download from the Sempervivophilia website. Correvon's treatise gives a good picture of the state of affairs in the semp world in the 1920s. Most of the species he describes are now known to be hybrids or color variants of existing species. It is a scholarly piece, though, with very good references and clear descriptions of the plants. Because these plants made it to this country through Carl Purdy, many of these names are associated with plants that were distributed throughout the US.

Eggli, U (2003) *Illustrated Handbook of Succulent Plants: Crassulaceae.* Springer. Berlin, Germany

This volume consists of collections of articles by experts in each of the genera of succulent plants in the Crassulaceae, including semps and sedums. The chapter on semps represents the current thinking on the status of the various species and is one where the genus *Jovibarba* is reduced to a section of the genus *Sempervivum*. It is the classification system used in this work. Although the title indicates there are lots of illustrations, there are relatively few, and they are clustered in plates toward the back of the book. This is not a coffee table picture book but a serious botanical work.

Wills, Howard and Sally (2004) *An Introduction to Sempervivum and Jovibarba Species and Cultivars.* Fernwood Nursery. Torrington, Devon, UK

This fifty-two page booklet is a superbly illustrated work that describes and pictures a number of species and cultivars. Almost all aspects of semps are briefly discussed, and this is an excellent beginner's book. Howard's enthusiasm for the group is obvious, and the illustrations of his plantings, pots, and beautifully staged collection make this a visual treat. Copies of this book and a CD containing more photos may be obtained from Fernwood Nursery. Before this version there were two previous versions, one covering the *Rosularia* group, as well. The coverage in each is a bit different, and if you can find them, all are useful additions to a semp enthusiast's library.

Haberer, M and Graf, H. (2010)
500 Winterharte Sukkulenten & Kakteen. Ulmer, Germany.

Although this book is written in German, there is relatively little text. Rather, there are lots of small photos of numerous semps included in this book, including a large selection of *S. heuffelii* cultivars grouped by color. One of the authors is a semp hybridizer of considerable importance, and it is not surprising that the coverage of semps is incredible. The book is also useful for those hunting for companion plants that are also winter hardy succulents. The coverage of hardy cactus and sedums is quite impressive.

Smith, AC (1975) *The Genus Sempervivum and Jovibarba.*
Published by author. Kenton, Kent, UK

This is a small pamphlet from an enthusiast and nursery owner. He inherited the collection of Praeger's plants from enthusiast Hugh Miller. This booklet gives details of these species and addresses more of the garden issues of these species than Praeger's monograph. In addition, newer species and some hybrids are given brief descriptions. Alan's description of the species have much less botanical jargon, and thus it is much more reader friendly than Praeger. Although I have a PhD in botany, it was not in taxonomy, so words like "acuminate" do not come easily off the tongue or register clearly in the brain.

Baldwin, DL (2007) *Designing with Succulents.*
Timber Press. Portland, Oregon

Although this book is mainly concentrated on warmer and dryer climates than where semps would be most happy, there is a chapter on more cold climate succulents. Debra's eye for landscaping though is something that oozes from all the pages of this book, and many of the concepts that she introduces can be used successfully in many situations involving semps, too.

Horvath, B (2014) *The Plant Lover's Guide to Sedums.* Timber Press. Portland, Oregon

Sedums are one of the great companion plants for semps, and this new book is a wonderful account of that group by a very successful hybridizer and nurseryman. He knows these plants well and walks you through the taxonomic changes that divide sedums into several new genera. Beautiful illustrations. After reading this, you will have a long list of companions for your semps.

Kelaidis, G (2008) *Hardy Succulents: Tough Plants for Every Climate.* Storey Publishing. Adams Massachusetts

Gwen Kelaidis writes with love about a variety of hardy succulent plants, including semps. The photos, most the work of Saxon Holt, are a beautiful complement to the text. The photos show ways in which hardy succulents may be used in garden situations and are thus especially useful in this regard. A semp is even on the cover!

Sedum Society Newsletter. Various Volumes.

Although this is a society for sedums, editor Ray Stephenson publishes articles on all of the Crassulaceae, and he has collected/examined many of the semp species growing in the wild. The volumes are published in England, but the society dues may be paid through an American member in dollars. Each of the issues (four per year) are roughly twenty-five pages, and a seed list is offered each year along with a cutting exchange. Another group worth joining that feature semps or related plants includes the North American Rock Garden Society. The journals are beautifully illustrated and an amazing seed list is available each year that always has some unique offerings.

WEBSITES

It is not surprising that much of the information on semps can be found on the internet now too. Several of these have very useful information, especially on lists of cultivars, and images of these will be helpful in determining wish lists for your garden.

The National Gardening Association (garden.org)

This website features a chat group that is overseen very ably by semp gurus Chris Rentmeister and Lynn Smith. Members of the group post comments, questions, and images that are just for the enjoyment of the group. A rather extensive set of photographs of cultivars is maintained by the group. "Semp police" continually go over these cultivar photos to make sure the cultivars are in fact correct. The substantial confusion of cultivars over the years, in which cultivars were sold under the wrong names, is slowly being corrected by this group of sleuths. This group has served as the nucleus for our annual "Hybridizers Clinic" that occurs in Oregon.

Sempervivophilia (sempervivophilia.stalikez.info)

This site was created by Gerard Dumont, and although originally written in French, there is an English translation. This site covers many aspects of semps: a good discussion of the cytology, evolution, and hybridization, plus a list of cultivars and their hybridizers. Lots of information and some things not found elsewhere in the literature are available on this site.

Sempervivum Liste (sempervivum-liste.de)

Our friend Peter Dieckmann was an obsessed collector of semps. Although he passed away several years ago, he has left a lasting legacy with this website. Nearly all of the cultivars and species clones are shown in photographs. Many of the plants are shown in different seasons, and for some of the cultivars pedigree information has been provided, as well details of the flowers. Several of his German colleagues have taken over for Peter, adding photos and data, as well as confirming identifications with hybridizers.

4mysemp (sites.google.com/site/4mysemp/sempervivum)

George Mendl has created a wonderfully fun site that has details of many aspects of semp folklore, culture, and propagation. The photos are really fun, and the text can be translated by Google translator for those not fluent in German.

Carlo deWilde (www.carlodewilde.nl)

Carlo gives a comprehensive list of the species and provides photos from his collection of representatives of some of these species. This is a good place to see how hybridizing has progressed compared to these progenitors.

SOURCES

USA
SMG Succulents

Don Mylin offers a wonderful variety of semps. His nursery has a direct line of history from Helen Payne's plants, and many of the classic as well as newer hybrids (some of them his own) are offered. SMG Succulents is a retail only nursery, and all selections are shown with color images on the SMG website. Collections are also available for those not able to decide on individual plants. Plants are shipped bare root.

Mountain Crest Gardens

Tom and Matts Jopson run Mountain Crest Gardens. Their plants from Irene Russ, a member of the Sempervivum Fancier's Association and Sempervivum Society, served as a basis of their sales plants, but they have also added plants from many other sources, as well. Mountain Crest offers a number of cultivars, with an especially fine collection of S. heuffelii cultivars. In addition, collections, fun pots, books on succulents, and even wreath material for making succulent wreaths are available. Besides semps, hardy Rosularia and Orystachys plants that are similar in morphology to semps are available. Plants are grown in pots. Very fun website.

Chris Rentmeister

Chris is from Wisconsin, and she offers a number of unusual cultivars from her personal collection. Many of these are new acquisitions from Europe and so are unique offerings in the US. Plants are well grown and are shipped bare root. Chris is one of the "identification police," so you can trust her names.

Perennial Obsessions

Cynda Foster and Dave Jerell maintain a large collection of semps grown in pots. Selections from their vast collection are offered each year online and in numerous plant sales around the Pacific Northwest. Cynda has special talents in putting together interesting arrangements and wreaths featuring semps and other hardy succulents. Some of these unique pieces are also available at plant sales.

Young's Garden Center

Toby Lander took a portion of the family garden center business and created a unique boutique online business. The website has beautiful photos of each offering, plus a good discussion of culture. Toby sends out bare root plants and includes a surprise extra with each order. Since 2014, he has listed the hybrids of Kevin Vaughn, both the new ones and more historic ones that still have merit.

Strong's Alpine Succulents

Although I do not know this dealer personally, they offer a nice selection of semps and other hardy succulents, including a few I have been looking to re-acquire. The nursery is at 7,000 ft., so the plants are really from an Alpine environment.

EUROPE

Erwin Geiger's Nursery

Erwin Geiger's website is an absolute fun place for semp lovers, as there are so many beautiful plants, including the cutting edge of new hybrids, plus what is considered the best of previous introductions. Erwin has introduced a number of outstanding cultivars of his own as well, and there are some especially nice smaller rosettes among these hybrids. Plants are shipped bare root.

Fernwood Nursery

Owner Howard Wills is a long time semp addict, and he was a friend of semp legend David Ford. Many of David's hybrids can still be found among Howard's listings, as well as many of the better English hybrids. Howard's hybrids 'Lion King' and 'Starburst' are particularly fine, as is his species selection of S. *calcareum* known as 'Extra.'